A GROWNUP GUIDE TO
EFFECTIVE CRANKINESS:
The CrankaTsuris Method

STEVEN JOSEPH

ARCHWAY
PUBLISHING

Archway Publishing books may be ordered through booksellers or by contacting:

Archway Publishing
1663 Liberty Drive
Bloomington, IN 47403
www.archwaypublishing.com
844-669-3957

Photography by JJ Ignotz Photography.
Interior Image Credit: Andy Case.
Shutterstock pictures - unlimited license, also pictures from The Last Surviving Dinosaur: The TyrantoCrankaTsuris, and personal pictures from author's catalogue.
Author Website at www.StevenJosephAuthor.com

ISBN: 978-1-4808-9381-8 (sc)
ISBN: 978-1-4808-9380-1 (hc)
ISBN: 978-1-4808-9382-5 (e)

Library of Congress Control Number: 2020921505

Print information available on the last page.

Archway Publishing rev. date: 10/29/2020

CONTENTS

DEDICATION

To Dan Goldwasser, who always told me that if you want to be an expert about something, you have to write about it. To Roshi Enkio Pat O'Hara, who taught me to embrace my own true nature. And to my wonderful daughter, Vita, who always reminds me to have a dream.

To my mother, Rose Joseph, a holocaust and cancer survivor who passed away in September 2017. And to my father, Rudy Joseph, who passed away in February 2020, who voiced the words "I love" every day. I was fortunate to have two special people as my parents.

And, a Special Thank You to Andy Case, who brought the TyrantaCrankaTsuris to life.

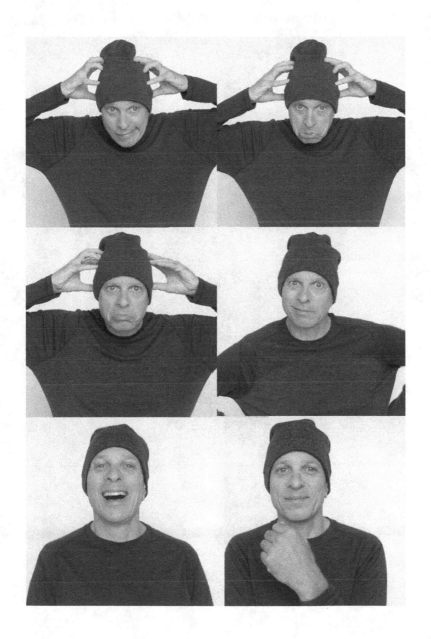

PROLOGUE
HOW TO USE YOUR OWN CRANKATSURIS

I wrote *The Last Surviving Dinosaur: The TyrantoCrankaTsuris* last year, as a kids' book. This book, however, was written not only with kids in mind. As the narrator says, "Even Mommy and Daddy can be a TyrantoCrankaTsuris and TyrantoKvetchaTsuris sometimes!" So, it is important for us to acknowledge our own "CrankaTsuris."

Imagine if a family member is standing on a very expensive rug. This close family member informs you that he or she is feeling very ill. You observe that this important person is in fact sick and is about to throw up. This sick person politely asks which way to the bathroom.

The response is never, "No. I insist that you do it right where you are standing! What better place for you to do it than on this rug. It is a priceless antique. The rug used to be on display at the Museum of Art. Do you know that this rug was on the floor of the main living room of Buckingham Palace? Of course, you have to know that you are standing close to my Picasso, as well. How about you try to shoot some of that outgoing projectile from your mouth that way? Do you think you can reach the Picasso? I can push you a bit closer, and I would consider it a bonus!"

Actually, the normal response is, "Not on the rug! It is a precious antique! Go to the bathroom! Do not worry. If you can't make it, I will just push you in!" Then the poor sickly member of the family rushes to the bathroom.

All of us are aware that all of our family members are much more important than the very expensive rug. Despite this, we typically do not hesitate to pour out our CrankaTsuris all over our spouses, kids, parents, and siblings—and then there can be a CrankaTsuris retaliation. Before you know it, you are in the middle of a CrankaTsuris food fight. When it is all over, just like the rug, it can be very difficult to clean up a CrankaTsuris.

So, we try to feel it coming. We feel it inside. It starts in the pit of our stomach, and it moves up to our throat. Instead of just letting it all out, stop for a couple of seconds and breathe. Warn the person you love so much that you have a CrankaTsuris inside and it may be coming. Say why you are feeling this CrankaTsuris inside you. Say what you may need to make it less messy. But, remember one thing. If you were not able to help yourself, and you did pour out a CrankaTsuris all over your loved one, apologize and say you had a little "CrankaTsuris" when you finally calm down.

So invite the TyrantoCrankaTsuris and the TyrantoKvetchaTsuris into your home. Begin with your own CrankaTsuris practice, and have fun with what is really our true nature!

THE STORY OF THE LAST SURVIVING DINOSAUR: THE TYRANTOCRANKATSURIS

"Tsuris" (pronounced tSSuris!!—light on the T, and very heavy on the S) is the Yiddish word for problems. Now, when I say "problems," I am not talking about a minor daily inconvenience. I am talking about a major, life-changing, traumatic event that has brought on such suffering that, never before, has ever been experienced by anyone since the beginning of time, and something you would never wish on your worst enemy.

Consider the difference in the two statements: "I have this problem" and "Oy! I have such tsuris! Oy!" While a problem is something you may choose to keep to yourself, tsuris is something you have to share with the entire world. Think of some real tsuris you may have, and try to keep it to yourself.

See! You cannot do it.

I grew up in a very Jewish home in the Bronx. My parents and the rest of my family came over from Europe after World War II. And, I can tell you this. My home was like many other Jewish homes, at least in my neighborhood. All the relatives would get together and start kvetching—talking about tsuris in a very competitive manner. "You think you have tsuris? If I had your tsuris, I would be doing cartwheels! Nobody can outdo my tsuris!"

We all talked about our tsuris with a huge sense of pride. For us, there was a feeling of real accomplishment. It was as if we were all training for the Olympics and tsuris was an Olympic event. One of us was going to get the gold!

"How are you doing, Aunt Saydie?"

"I am okay, but I have these warts on my toes, and I can't get rid of them!"

My second cousin Dottie would chime in. "I would take the warts! I got my warts removed, and my toenails fell off! And the fungus between the toes—there is serious vegetation growing there!"

Aunt Sandy would lean herself over and proudly say, "Oy! But both of you did not go through what I went through! I went to Florida and then, was bit by an alligator! Look at me now! I am turning into a reptile!"

Sure enough, Aunt Sandy had grown alligator feet with scales and claws that had a nice nail polish gold and purple finish. Aunt Saydie and cousin Dottie examined the alligator feet, and they were very impressed indeed.

On the other side of the room, the men would be talking.

"How are you doing, Uncle Mottie?"

"I could be better. For years, I thought I had this terrible problem with dandruff—used every brand of dandruff shampoo. Nothing helped. I finally found out it was lice. I am a walking plague!"

My cousin Whiny would interrupt. "Don't tell me about lice. I never leave the city. I stay on concrete. I do not even go into a park. Do you know what happened to me? I got ticks—deer ticks! Only I can get deer ticks in Brooklyn!"

Uncle Shmukie, with his booming voice, would grab the gold: "I would take lice and ticks in a heartbeat! I just got back from the doctor. Do you know what this doctor told me? I have an inoperable brain tumor. The doctor says it is not life threatening, but it is a brain tumor! The doctor put a magnetic metal plate around the brain tumor to keep it from growing. Now, they will not let me fly on airplanes. They think I am carrying a bomb inside my head!"

Just to show off Uncle Shmukie's magnetism, he took out a box of paper clips, and placed it on the table. Sure enough, as he put his head closer to the table, all the paper clips flew up to the top of his head!

So this all prepared me very well when I became a father and my daughter had a temper tantrum. I put her in time-out. But, I told her that when she came out, I would tell her the real story about how most, but not all, of the dinosaurs became extinct.

My daughter then thought to herself, *this should be a good story!* She quietly composed herself while in her bedroom. When the time-out was over, she said, "I'm ready for the story, Daddy! Wait! You said that not all dinosaurs are extinct. That is not what I learned in school!"

"It isn't true. One small dinosaur survived. Even though she was the smallest dinosaur, she was the most dangerous of all. And believe it or not, we humans are her ancestors. We all are descendants from this one little tiny dinosaur," I said.

"What was the name of this dinosaur?" my daughter asked, her interest piqued.

"The TyrantoCrankaTsuris!"

"I've never heard of that dinosaur," my daughter replied.

With a mischievous smile, I began to tell her the story. "The TyrantoCrankaTsuris was the smallest dinosaur on the planet, and all of the other dinosaurs made fun of her because of her size. The other dinosaurs liked to brag about how tough they were!

'I can eat an entire forest with one bite!' one said.

"A second dinosaur exclaimed, 'My teeth are so big, they are the size of an entire forest!'

"A third dinosaur boasted, 'I floss my teeth with an entire forest!'

"And they all made fun of and laughed at the little TyrantoCrankaTsuris, until one day, the little TyrantoCrankaTsuris got really, really mad at the other dinosaurs and let out the biggest and loudest CrankaTsuris:

'I have bad warts on my toes that do not come off, but they came off and my toenails came off with them, and then I grew fungus the size of an entire forest. So I went to Florida to soak my forest feet in the ocean, and an alligator bit off my forest feet, but it bit my feet too—and it hurt so much!'

"And with that CrankaTsuris, the whole planet shook and went dark. However, the TyrantoCrankaTsuris did not stop.

"'And then I couldn't stop scratching my scales, and I thought I had dandruff, but it was really lice, and then I found out I had deer ticks even though deer do not exist in prehistoric times, and I can't get the deer ticks removed because I have an inoperable brain tumor, and if they tried to remove the deer ticks, my brains would splatter all over, and my head would really hurt even worse!'

"She went on and on and on, cranking out all of her tsuris that she had suffered her entire life until all of the bigger and badder dinosaurs on the planet had vanished—all except one.

The TyrantoCrankaTsuris met another tiny dinosaur: the TyrantoKvetchaTsuris. When he arrived from Florida with the alligator he captured, they fell in love. They soon got married and cranked and kvetched happily ever after. Millions of years later, these last two dinosaurs evolved into humans.

"Before, you were getting a bit cranky and kvetchy. That is the part that we humans inherited from the TyrantoCrankaTsuris and the TyrantoKvetchaTsuris. Even Mommy and Daddy can be a TyrantoCrankaTsuris and TyrantoKvetchaTsuris!

"You need to be careful with this power," I told my daughter. "Remember, all of the other dinosaurs became extinct when the TyrantoCrankaTsuris just would not stop!

So we learned to be careful not to express our inner TyrantoCrankaTsuris or TyrantoKvetchaTsuris too often—just the right amount to keep the planet happy and not too cranky."

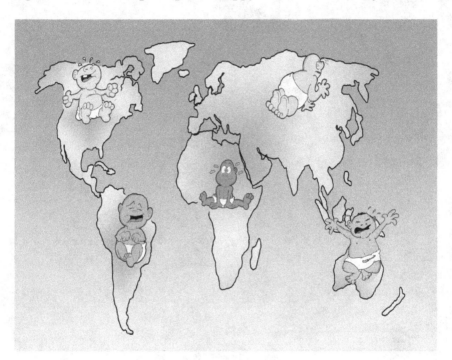

THE CRANKATSURIS METHOD

The premise behind the idea of CrankaTsuris is that crankiness is part of our true nature. Think about it! We are the only species that enter this world crying. You would not see a litter of puppies or kittens being born and wailing away the second they enter this world.

Even chickens do not cry when they are born and hatch out of their shells. If I were a chicken, when I come out of my shell, I would definitely cry my head off!

They emerge from their cozy temperature controlled shell into a crowded chicken pen. Obviously, they forgot to think about social distancing. Once they are out of their shell, their parents then give them weird names like "Rotisserie" or "Cupasoup." At least for me, this sounds like the perfect recipe for chickens to start screaming their head off.

Imagine that you are in a deep sleep in your nice cozy bed, and when you wake up, you are stuck on the A train during rush hour.

I do not have to imagine since this has been an actual experience of mine. Not fun at all.

Now, animals do cry, of course. However, it is mostly from real suffering. When my daughter was growing up, we had a fabulous mutt of a dog, Albus Dumbledog. If there was a thunderstorm or if he was dealing with some serious bathroom issues and wanted to go out to relieve himself, his cries would let us know. He would not start crying because we turned off his favorite TV show on Animal Planet.

We can get cranky just because we do not get our own way, especially when we are young. Even when we get old, we may get cranky for the same reason, but we may show it in a passive-aggressive fashion. We may act out in a way that could be harmful not only to our loved ones but also to ourselves.

The answer, that all of us have been told, was to not act out. Rather, we should just say what we are feeling, as if by saying it, we can make the feeling go away. We should just verbalize. "Johnny, if you are angry, you can say that you are angry. That is a lot better than hitting Tommy!"

While saying what we feel is obviously a better choice than acting out, think about this for a moment. Imagine that we become experts at saying what we feel: "I feel angry." "I feel mad." "I feel annoyed." "I feel irritated." There is also a physical aspect to this. My blood pressure goes up. I feel a rush of adrenaline. Maybe, I take a physical action: eating. I will drown my sorrows with a bowl of ice cream—no, not a bowl … a quart of ice cream with toppings.

The physical part is still there. If I keep on saying on a daily basis, "I feel angry," for example, I may at some point start to believe I am this very angry person. Not only that, because I am always telling you about my angry feelings, despite the fact that you appreciate that I tell that I am angry, you end up believing that I am a very angry person.

"Our son Johnny is such an angry boy! I am so pleased that he tells us how angry he is. There was that one day that Johnny forgot to tell me how angry he was. That was a scary day. Believe me. I was so worried."

Here the CrankaTsuris comes in to save the day. You have a loved one who is feeling the edge and may want to verbalize hurtful things. A little kid wants to hit his brother because he is playing with the toy that is only his—no sharing! Now, we want to preserve all of the goodness, sweetness, kindness, and lovingness of that person. We do not want to label that person as a bad person. We can avoid that sort of negative outcome by rolling up those feelings into a CrankaTsuris.

Johnny is not an angry boy. He just is a sweet kid with a little CrankaTsuris in him.

There is a CrankaTsuris stuck in our throats. We do not say how we are feeling but just that we have a CrankaTsuris. The CrankaTsuris will pass. Think about what works. It can be different for everybody. Some may want a quiet space. Others can ask for permission to let out a big CrankaTsuris. We can make it a reward for kids for good behavior. Others may want to have fun and be a TyrantoCrankaTsuris.

Now, what does a CrankaTsuris sound like? It can be a dinosaur roar. Maybe, it can be just the very long string of complaints you have sitting inside you. You can begin to shout out all the little things that did not go your way that day:

> "My coffee was cold. I missed the train. It was too crowded. Oh, this guy next to me on the train was smelly. Did I tell you my boss gave me extra work? I want to strangle him! Can you believe there are some people who do not believe in flushing a toilet? I spent three hours on hold with the insurance company! Of course, they were useless! Just look at me now! With this humidity, my hair is an absolute nightmare. The pimple is just getting bigger and bigger— probably from all this humidity! Now I have to cook dinner.

*What do you mean you forgot to go to the grocery store? I
am so tired!"*

Let out all of your CrankaTsuris, and do not stop until you start
laughing and are unable to stop laughing. You do it as a performance.
Keep going with family members there, and do not stop until they
all vanish—not permanently, of course!

There is one important rule with the CrankaTsuris: do not attack
any family member. It is not about putting any loved one down. It is
about the little things in life that tend to end up rolled up in a big ball.

When you start to crack yourself up, it means that you have
wrapped the CrankaTsuris in a nice big ball inside your throat. You
can then go to the sink and spit it out. Gargle a bit just to make sure
you feel cleansed, and then everybody can come back, since it is nice
and safe again.

When you are all done, say something good, something that is
a constant: "I get home, and I have my beautiful family." "It smells
so good."

It is all about making it light and making it fun. We need to
make it about that tiny dinosaur we all descended from: the
TyrantoCrankaTsuris!

3

CRANKATSURIS GAMES

"And the TyrantoCrankaTsuris went on and on, cranking out the tsuris until all the bigger, badder dinosaurs had vanished."

It is great to be so small, to have everyone be bigger and badder than you—and you have all the power. You are the most dangerous dinosaur on the planet. So much fun!

This part of the story came from the simple game of tag with my daughter and her friends on the playground when she was young. It would not be as much fun if we had just played it straight and I was one of the kids.

Because I was obviously bigger than all the young ones, the game of tag always started out as me playing the monster, trying to capture them. I would always get really, really close and then just miss getting them.

I would only come close to making a capture if I got bored, or tired. Because I never really caught any of the kids, the game, at some point, would have to change. I became the scared monster, and all the kids would chase me. I became terrified, yelping and crying for my momma with my arms waving.

I must have done this so often that I became a professional scaredy-cat monster. Little kids could smell me a mile away. Years later, I went to Israel to visit cousins. My cousins had little children, who did not speak English, and I did not speak Hebrew. I would sit innocently with the other grown-ups, having a grown-up conversation. Right in the middle of the conversation, these little four-year-old kids would come up to me, and say, in their Israeli kid accent, "Roar!" The chase was on. I could never say "no" to such cute kids.

Last year, I was at Tanglewood for the July 4 concert James Taylor concert. During intermission, the same thing happened. A little kid sitting with the family on the blanket next to us looked at me and gave me that instinctive roar. I must have run five miles during intermission. Afterwards, I got offers to babysit from not only that kid's parents, but also from three other families! It was too bad the pay was not that good.

So, you can do this. If your kid gets a bit too cranky, stick him or her in a time-out, and after they are calm and well behaved for a while, reward them! Let them be the TyrantoCrankaTsuris, and they can chase you around, cranking out all their tsuris!

Of course, you never disappear.

Know what is even better that this? What if Mom and Dad had a bad day and they are feeling a bit cranky? You get to take turns and switch places! How much fun is that!

CHAPTER 4

CRANKATSURIS QUARANTINE

Here is a crazy hypothetical. Imagine that a crazy worldwide pandemic hits the entire planet. Stay at home orders are in place to fight the pandemic. We are now in week whatever with the stay at home orders. Families are all stuck together twenty-four hours a day in quarantine.

This is what I like to compare this crazy hypothetical to:

The family is going on a long vacation to Disney World. They are driving from New York to Florida, and they are all stuck together packed in the minivan. Both of the kids are suffocating in the back. They are both crushed between the suitcases. Crumbs of potato chips and cheese doodles cover the seats and the floor. The baby's diaper needs to be changed. The smells permeate the car. She begins to scream her head off.

At least, they are going on the vacation the family had planned for years. When the kids are cranking out, "Are we there yet?" the grown-ups in the car actually have some idea when they plan to arrive at the Magic Kingdom.

Because of the "stay at home" orders, there is no Magic Kingdom destination. It is not just the kids asking the question, "are we there yet?" Everyone in the family is asking the same question, and nobody in the family has even a clue on what the answer can be.

With all the big unknowns, and with nobody knowing exactly the answer to "Are we there yet?" there is fear, frustration, and of course, crankiness. Because of fear of the unknown, and the frustration of being prisoners in our own home, now is the perfect time to have all the family members work on their "effective" crankiness.

If you think about "effective crankiness," think of something you are creating that can be described as home grown, hand crafted, artisanal, all natural, no artificial ingredients added—and most importantly, however,—not free of pesticides (because we all can be pests once in a while). The only other thing we cannot be at this time, unfortunately, is cage free.

Therefore, "effective crankiness" is the development of our inner "CrankaTsuris." I coined the word "CrankaTsuris" because I wanted to make the concept of crankiness have a physical three-dimensional feel to it. When we are feeling cranky, and our crankiness does not have any physical aspect to it, this crankiness becomes the invisible enemy that takes us by surprise. Invisible enemies, it turns out, happen to be scarier than the enemies we can see. Think of "ineffective crankiness" like a teakettle with boiling water. One second, the teakettle looks like a teakettle, and the next second, the top explodes off.

The crankiness explosion creates this feeling of one person feeling like the bad person, and the other person not feeling very safe. The perfect example is the explosions toward a loved one on something that person does or says with a good amount of frequency. Partner A does X, and for nine times, it does not bother Partner B a bit. One time, it even made Partner B laugh. Then, the tenth time comes around, and Partner B explodes at what Partner A did.

Look what Partner B did. Partner A is looking at Partner B being very hurt because not only did Partner B attack Partner A verbally, Partner B did two other things. Partner B attacked Partner A without warning. It was a surprise attack. Second, the first nine times did not bother Partner B a bit. Because of this, when Partner B went on the attack the tenth time around, it was such a shock that causes Partner A to no longer feel safe in this situation, or any other situation.

Partner B also feels terrible, but also, is somewhat confused. Partner B was not irritated at the first nine times, but now that Partner A is angry, Partner B wants a trophy for not getting upset for those first nine times. Partner B is now angry at Partner A's reaction. Partner B completely misses the point that the surprise attack has caused mistrust with Partner A.

Utilizing the CrankaTsuris Method, what could Partner A and Partner B have done differently? If we think about this crankiness as a physical three-dimensional object inside us, we can think a bit on how to control it. Do I really want to do a projectile vomit all over the brand new couch that someone I love happens to be sitting on? I really do not. When I know it has a physicality to it, I can warn somebody that I happen to have a CrankaTsuris in me. "I am feeling tired and depleted, and I have to warn everyone I have a CrankaTsuris coming!" Once everyone embraces the concept of a CrankaTsuris,—even if one person who has it is unable to stop it,—the partner can recognize that it was a CrankaTsuris. It was something that everyone gets.

Because of this, what happens? Well, if Partner B lets out a CrankaTsuris, and both partners get good practice at it, Partner B's CrankaTsuris has nothing to do with and is not about Partner A. It is just about Partner B being cranky. It becomes okay to be cranky and embrace our crankiness. It also is not about making Partner A feel bad for what Partner A said or did. It is not about Partner A feeling less safe and less trusting of Partner B. You can have something very special when everybody feels safe and trusting, even when things get a little hard.

Well, in these quarantined times, we need to practice on our organized CrankaTsuris. Who gets to perform their CrankaTsuris?

Does the family get to embrace it? Do the kids get to play the scary TyrantoCrankaTsuris monster, and the grownups run away all scared while the kids are in hysterics? Do we allow for quiet moments when they are exactly what we need for our crankiness? Create a CrankaTsuris Family Schedule, or even a Family CrankaTsuris checklist.

"So, we learned to be careful not to express our inner TyrantoCrankaTsuris or TyrantoKvetchaTsuris too often. Just the right amount to keep the planet happy, and not too cranky."

...But if we do, let us have some fun with it!

CRANKATSURIS INTROVERT

"And the TyrantoCrankaTsuris went on and on, cranking out the tsuris until all the bigger, badder dinosaurs had vanished."

Now, in truth, the TyrantoCrankaTsuris was always the quiet one. However, as they always say, "It's the quiet ones that you have to watch out for."

It is a fact that some people never like to complain. I never trust them! Let me tell you a story. At work, I had a former colleague; I call him Vic. It was because his name was Vic. Every morning I would see him in the coffee room, and I would ask, "Vic, how are you doing?"

"I can't complain," he would always reply. "What kind of answer is that?" I thought to myself. I was asking how he was doing. I did not ask the question if he had the ability to complain. Imagine if I asked Vic how he was doing and he said, "I can't swim." There is no difference in the two nonanswers.

There is another thing that I want to tell you about Vic. See! I am complaining! This is the same person, who on Friday mornings, when he would see me in the coffee room, would say to me, "Steve, if I don't see you, you should have a good weekend!" Now we worked in the same department, and I was not going anywhere. I was going to be there for another seven hours. Of course, Vic would see me. Did that mean I should have a lousy weekend?

I digressed a bit. Some people just do not like to complain. Yet, think about why they do not like to complain. They say, "I don't want to seem like a complainer!" They might say, "What's the point? I can complain, but it will not change anything!"

One reason you will never ever hear is, "I do not complain because there is absolutely nothing to complain about. Everything is just perfect. I am completely satisfied with absolutely everything. OK, there is one thing. I am underworked and over-appreciated, but that's it—no other complaints!"

We all have our complaints. Now imagine if we chose not to voice our complaints. Let us presume that the reason we do not complain is exactly that it will not change anything. Do you know what will then happen? Nothing will ever change, because there was never anyone to complain about the way it was. If there is nobody to complain, we must all be living in a perfect world.

The problem with this kind of thinking is that we do need change. Things are not perfect. Complaining is showing bravery. It creates change. I will tell you a short story that brings it full circle. When I was young, and I was really hoping for something to happen. I really wanted to get that acceptance letter from my first choice for college. My father told me, "Don't get your hopes up. That way, you will not be disappointed."

My father said many wise things that fathers always say, but I did not put that line into the category of "wise fatherly sayings." So what if I am disappointed? I worked hard. I think I deserve what I worked hard to get. If I do not get it, I will be disappointed. That is OK. I will not let this disappointment crush me, but it will motivate me to work harder. I have something to prove.

Complaining is not just OK. It is both important and vital to our existence and even our survival as human beings. People complain, and they experience disappointment when things do not change. However, the best of us do not give up. We keep on fighting. At some point, there will be someone there to hear our complaints, and answer them as well.

It is important to remember. We do not keep it in, keep it in, keep it in, and then let it out and never stop. Nobody hears the TyrantoCrankaTsuris who never stops cranking out the tsuris.

And, the story ends: "So we learned to be careful not to express our inner TyrantoCrankaTsuris or TyrantoKvetchaTsuris too often—just the right amount to keep the planet happy and not too cranky."

CHAPTER 6

DRIVER'S ED CRANKATSURIS

People would come to me, and ask me about effective versus ineffective crankiness, and when I try to explain, some like to argue with me that there is no such thing as ineffective crankiness.

Often, some wise guy tells me the following: "You know what? I just want to blow off some steam. When I blow off a little steam, I feel a whole lot better. There's nothing wrong with that!"

Yes. We absolutely have to blow off some steam. But, do you know what? Steam is always hot. Steam can still burn. Who are you to be the expert on what is the exact amount of steam to blow off? Do you let a bunch of steam pile up inside before blowing a ton of steam? Maybe you let just a small amount of steam blow off. You think that if you blow a tiny amount of steam, that will help you ease the pressure a bit.

….Who do you blow the steam on? Let us say you blew so much steam you need to take back some of the steam. Do you know how to do that? Then let us say you blew off some steam on someone who did not want the steam and already complained about the humidity. Let us say that the person who you blew steam on starts blowing their own steam on you.

You say that you finally needed to blow off steam, and the second you blow off the steam, someone blows a whole bunch of steam right on you. The person had their steam mixed with your steam, so when this person blew steam on you, you ended up with twice the amount of steam that you started with!

Now because you have twice the amount of steam, and you were not able to handle half the amount, you start blowing off all the extra steam. The cycle continues until we have a serious global warming situation. All the ice caps begin to melt, and our civilization ceases to exist. Just because you wanted to blow your teensy weensy bit of steam! Oy!

"So, tell me. You couldn't afford to go to a sauna or a steam room for a little schvitz? It costs ten dollars for a half an hour. Next time, if you have a problem, let me know, and I will lend you the money."

The answer is that we never really know the exact right amount. That is why I talk about training ourselves by putting all of our crankiness into this CrankaTsuris. Once we visualize this physical blob inside of us, we can then decide when, where, and how to deposit it. While you do it, you can think of yourself as a chef, and take a little taste. It may need a little sugar, or it may need a pinch of salt. You get to play with it until it tastes just right. Now, you can go and blow the steam effectively.

"Cooking in the kitchen" is a fun and useful metaphor when thinking about this, but that is only when you have become a decent cook. My favorite one for beginners to use is "Driver's Ed School."

Now, when I talk about Driver's Ed School, I am not talking about a kid who has Dad and Mom around to take them out for lessons. These kids get to drive on empty country roads. They practice in empty parking lots. They get to drive in 21st Century cars of today that have that go-kart quality to them.

No. I am not talking about the unique experience that I alone had. This was the same experience that all my friends had when learning how to drive in the Bronx in the mid-to-late 1970s. It was a different and unique experience from anyone else's, except maybe the kids from Brooklyn.

The kids from Bronx drove on the Grand Concourse and Moshlou Parkway. The kids from Brooklyn drove on Coney Island Avenue and Ocean Parkway. Of course, I am sure the kids from Brooklyn had their own marvelous adventures!

You may wonder, *Why is it that this New York City 1970s kid's experience is so different?* My answer is *everything.*

First, you have to understand that my parents did not know how to drive. They took the train and the bus. I never thought anything bad or ashamed of that fact because none of my friends' parents was able to drive either. We were all going to learn on our own.

Now, we would have to go to Driver's Ed School. This was not going to be the hour long "one-on-one' private session. Only some lucky rich kid in the suburbs got their parents to pay for that. No. We could only afford to do the much less expensive group lessons. My friends, Little Stewie and Big Al, and I reserved three months of lessons on Thursday afternoons at four o'clock. We went to Bronx High School of Science and walked over to the Catholic School nearby, Cardinal Spellman, to meet our teacher. The four of us were all equally terrified. We were scared to death because our lives would soon come crashing to an end with all of us trapped in a flaming two-ton fireball.

Think about this for a second. Our situation was not unique. This was standard for other kids as well. So, imagine that every afternoon in the Bronx, exactly when rush hour was about to start, hundreds of student drivers would hit the road. People, who worked in the Bronx, or just drove in the Bronx, knew that if they got out from work at four o'clock, they did not want to be on the road at four o'clock. This is because on top of the crazy cab drivers, unlicensed drivers, and city buses, you were going to run into the hundreds of cars with the Student Driver sign placed on top of the car.

We would witness a traffic jam every week, and sure enough, it was a six-car collision with three student driver cars.

"Oops. I guess someone else didn't make it this week!"

Because of this, you still got traffic. The other important reason there was all this traffic was none of the student drivers went faster than four or five miles an hour. I can tell you one thing, that when you are sixteen years old, you do not have a clue at what you are doing. Traffic is that teenager's best friend.

We also drove slowly because the equally terrified Driver's Ed teacher had two important rules. Press on the gas pedal gently, and press on the brake pedal as hard as you can.

In fact, I remember our first three lessons were the same. We did not actually drive. We just sat in a parking spot, practicing stepping on the gas and brake pedals.

I forgot to mention this part. Our driver instructor never taught driving lessons before. We were his lucky first students!

Eventually, we would drive slowly and carefully, squeezing the wheel as if we were expecting juice to come out of it. Be aware that these cars were from the 1970s, and they always would shake, rattle, and roll. We had a hard time figuring out that if I turned at the wheel a bit to the left, the car would go a lot to the left.

Minutes into my lesson, I started to scream:

"So, when do I turn the wheel all the way to the left? When do I turn it back to center? How do I know the wheel is back in the center? Oh no! I turned back all the way to the right. It is going right. Now, how do I straighten it out? I do not know how to straighten out the car. Now, we are going too far to the left! We are going to crash. I cannot find the brake pedal. I can't even feel my foot!"

Finally, the Driver's Ed teacher shouted the most beautiful words a teenager with three other lives in his hands could hear; "Pull over!" When that fails, he takes control with his own driving wheel, pedal and brake, and gets us safely pulled over. *Whew*!

I then leave the driver's seat with all the blood removed from my face, shaking, and completely in shock. I crumpled up in the back seat. My two friends, Little Stewie and Big Al, then got their turn to do the same.

We all survived this wonderful experience. We did not kill any of the old ladies crossing the street. We did not destroy any parked cars! Yes. We did learn various curse words in four, maybe five different languages. Yes. I understand that our Driver's Ed School teacher quit his job immediately thereafter. Apparently, he found a safer vocation. He signed up with the Marine Corps. I actually heard that he became a Navy Seal.

The important thing is that, amazingly, we all got our driver's license after all of that.

The story does not end just there though. Oh no. You have to understand that the kids all got their licenses when the parents did not know how to drive. The thing that happened with me was the exact same thing that happened with all of my friends. All of our fathers would get jealous, and demand that we teach them how to drive. Of course, none of the fathers wanted to bother with Driver's Ed School. They already paid for our school, and they expected that we would become the teachers. I did not realize at the time that when we got our driver's license, we would be simultaneously getting the Driver's Ed teaching license as well.

At least, my father did not make me take the written part. He did ask, and he did take me with him to the Department of Motor Vehicles so that he could possibly cheat after he failed the first time. I can say proudly that my father did pass on his own, and there was no cheating involved.

If learning how to drive in the Bronx was a terrifying experience, teaching our fathers how to drive was the same terrifying experience on steroids. Yes. We did try to take our fathers to learn to drive in an empty parking lot, but that never worked out.

"I paid for your lessons to drive on city streets, and you think you can teach me in a parking lot? What kind of son do I have? I want to drive on the highway!"

"And, don't close your eyes when I drive! Why are you so nervous? You know that you are just making me nervous!"

Yes. My father's first driving lesson was on Interstate 95. We went right on to the passing lane.

My eyes were closed shut the entire time.

We all survived, and while my father and all of our fathers got their driver's licenses, we all must have been terrible teachers because they were all terrible drivers. However, that is another story.

This is the point. When I talk about effective crankiness, the CrankaTsuris is the car we drive. It is because we all want to blow off some of the steam deep inside; the CrankaTsuris is never about driving two hundred miles per hour at a NASCAR race. Sometimes, we go to the left, and sometimes to the right, and sometimes, we just have to pull over.

Just remember this. With developing our CrankaTsuris muscles, we really do need to teach each other. It is because when we get into the CrankaTsuris car, sometimes we are the driver. At the same time, we also will be the passenger.

CRANKATSURIS COMFORT FOOD: MY MOM'S LATKE RECIPE

When kids have a CrankaTsuris in them, it is not always about having a bad day; it could be that the Cranksters in your home are just getting a bit hungry.

I wish I had asked my mom for some of her recipes. She made the best gefilte fish (ground-up boiled carp, with eggs, salt (no sugar), onion, and carrots). That dish can be enjoyable for a particular taste—and let us face it; it is a big process to make it. You have to buy the fish. You have to have a special grinder. You have to refrigerate it for hours after you make it. It has fish jelly that looks like phlegm. You add spicy red horseradish to it. If you were brave enough to make gefilte fish, and lucky enough that your kids would eat it, you would become a CrankaTsuris after you had finished the entire daylong adventure of making it.

I will give you something easier: my mom's potatoes latkes (also called potato pancakes). You can make them in fifteen to twenty minutes, depending on how many potatoes you use. You will need a food processor or mini-chopper that has a grate setting. Then, once your kids have a few of these latkes, they will wash the dishes, scrub the floors, and clean their rooms. These are the world's best latkes.

I see that I have your interest. Now, let me first explain why all the other latkes are terrible and do not make the cut. I do not even understand them. Imagine that you want to try a latke. You think that the best place to go and have this delicious latke is a nearby Jewish deli or restaurant. You are a tourist coming to New York, and this was on your "to do" list.

This is what I did. First, let me be clear. This was for investigative purposes only. I already had considered myself the self-proclaimed King of the Latke. I went to the Carnegie Deli. Together with the giant pastrami chopped liver triple decker sandwich that I had been craving for since my days in Pittsburgh, I ordered the giant potato latka. This giant latka was one of those giant potato disks that was oily, tasted old, and was definitely too chewy. They must have put some flour or matzah meal in them, so they tasted a bit cakey in a bad way. I did not know exactly what it was. The restaurant put something in them that ruined the experience.

My mom's recipe is very simple: one medium to large-size potato, one egg per potato, a slice of onion, salt to taste, and a touch of garlic powder (optional)—that is it.

However, there are a few things to know. I was always a purist, and for years, I hand grated the potato and onion. This would cause knuckle skin to go into the mix. I would joke afterwards that this was the most important ingredient. You needed knuckle skin for taste. I walked around with bloody knuckles for many of the years because I grated my latkes. My friends would always try to get me to use an appliance, and I refused. My family never pushed this because they knew better. It was always my friends that would ask my why should I suffer with bloody knuckles. I looked at them with horror. The potato has to be hand grated, or it just would not be the same. I can be stubborn sometimes.

One day, when no one was around (and it had to be when no one was around, just for the sake of my pride), I tried the mini-chopper. Let me tell you, it was a life changer. It costs maybe thirty dollars, and I no longer need to go to the hospital to get blood infusions anymore! Within seconds, you get a perfectly grated potato.

It is important to mix the egg and grated onion before you add the potato. The onion is for taste, but it is also for appearance. If you do not have the onion in there, and the potato gets grated and sits in a bowel with the egg, the mixture turns gray. This will happen if you are making a large batch with four or more potatoes. You will not have an attractive latke.

Once you have the mix all prepared, heat the oil in the nonstick frying pan until the oil gets hot and then spoon the batter into the frying pan in disk-like shapes. The latkes will attach to each other, so make sure you separate each latke from another latke. When you see a hint of brown crunch at the edges, start flipping the latkes over. Cook for a short while longer, and then lift them off and onto a tray. Use a paper towel to remove the excess oil. You are done!

Now taste them. The outside has an amazing light and subtle crunch. The inside is creamy and just melts in your mouth. It is humanly impossible to be suffering from CrankaTsuris while eating them—unless, of course, you eat about twenty and get a bit of a tummy ache.

Here is another trick. You can use this trick on Valentine's Day. This trick may also be used just to give it the old-fashioned bloody knuckle skin color. You can even dip your knuckles in the grated beet juice to give it a nice bloody look just to show you used the old knuckle skin recipe.

All you have to do is to add a slice or two of peeled beet (not a whole beet, but no more than a quarter of a medium sized beet) to the potato mixture. The batter will be nice and pink, and you will have awesome reddish latkes with the same great flavor. That is another way to tell your Cranksters at home how much you love them! While you watch them eat the latkes, you will see the CrankaTsuris melt away.

8

THE CRANKATSURIS DIET (OR THE PICKLED HERRING DIET AND OTHER CONVERSATIONS ON GETTING TO NORMAL)

December 1987.

This is nothing to do with my dinosaur friends, or even crankiness ... but here is the short version of the story together with its ending.

OK, but first, it has everything to do with crankiness. This was the moment in my life that I hit the peak of crankiness!

In December 1987, I hit 240 pounds. I got to dress as Santa Claus at my law firm Christmas party. Three weeks later, after losing my girl, my car and my job, I decided that I could not take that kind of weight anymore.

I determined that I was going to change my life. I switched from triple-decker sandwiches with pastrami and chopped liver to pickled herring. By June 1988, I had dropped eight-five pounds and cut nine inches off my waist. I went from a forty-inch waist to a thirty-one inch waist in those six months.

However, there is much more to this story.

I grew up in a Jewish home, and my mom was a wonderful cook. Everything my mom made was delicious. There was no boiled tongue, or stuffed derma served in my house. In fact, if I went to a bar mitzvah, and they served boiled tongue and stuffed derma, do you know what I did? I walked out.

The only problem was that she cooked a lot and wanted her two sons to eat a lot. When I brought my roommate home from college for a weekend, he asked me after dinner, "Do you always eat three meals a day, even if they are five minutes apart?"

Actually, we did not eat three meals five minutes apart. If my recollection serves me correctly, it was much closer to six.

As I said, my mom was a wonderful cook. Let me change that. She was an amazing cook. Everything she made tasty both silky and savory. Foods were prepared with a touch of salt or a touch of sugar. But, it was never used to dominate the food. My mom only used salt and sugar as the invitation to the delightful tastes that would await us.

I have to walk you through the daily event of dinner and you will understand. The first course was the appetizer. The big difference in my home was that there were always a number of appetizers offered. The appetizers alone could have been an entire two meals.

Certain appetizers were available seven days a week. A jar of pickled herring was first thing brought to the table. Then, a bowl of eggplant salad would be placed next to the pickled herring.

My mom always made fresh eggplant salad. This was simple, but it was also delicious. I still make it today. All it takes is a roasted eggplant with the eggplant meat finely chopped. Then, my mom would add chopped onion and garlic, a bit of salt, oil and lemon. My father worked at F & O Meat Plant in the South Bronx. That happened to be close to the D'Agostino Italian Bakery Factory, and it was there that my father came home daily with a hot fresh Italian bread. The eggplant salad made its way on to the bread, and we were already in heaven.

My mom made other appetizers that showed up to accompany the delicious hot bread. The two dishes that made a welcome appearance two to three times on a weekly basis was the home made chopped liver, and chicken fricassee. If we had chopped liver, my mom also served what she called "chicken candy." I think that was only fried chicken skin, or chicken fat. Whatever it was, it was delicious.

My mom used only chicken wings for the fricassee, and I am certain that my mom's chicken fricassee would blow away any Buffalo chicken wing today. There was a lot of turmeric and paprika used. We would also find the silky strips of onion, and bits of garlic. A little tomato paste was added in to help make an incredible sauce. The sauce, orange in color, was amazing for dipping the bread in. We used as much bread as we could to clean the plate.

Friday nights were always special because my mom would then bring out her homemade gefilte fish. Those unfortunate people, who have only experienced only jarred gefilte fish, will not be able to understand. It was only beyond heaven. The only way I can explain it is this way: There is sushi, and then, there is sushi. Anybody who has experienced amazing sushi will understand what I am saying.

After the appetizers, my mom served the salad. It was always simple. It consisted of iceberg lettuce, onion, cucumbers, peppers and tomatoes. The only dressing I ever knew was oil, salt and lemon. It actually was refreshing after the servings of bread and the condiments.

The soup was next. My father, in particular, loved soup. Because of this, he made it mandatory that for every dinner, there had to be soup. Of course, my mom made the best soups. The two soup headliners were my mom's matzah ball soup, and her vegetable soup. My mom expertly cleared the oil and Schmutz floating on the top of the boiling soup until it was a clear golden color. The matzah balls, carrots and onions all added to the velvety experience. The vegetable soup did the same.

All I can say is that the aftertaste of these two soups were pure pleasure.

Shortly after that, the main dish was placed on display. My mom loved making latkas. The latkas would release an intoxicating smell about two hours before dinner. I think my mom did that on purpose so that, by the time dinner was ready, we would be fully committed to a fifteen-course meal.

For the main course, my mom always had the Jewish/Eastern European food greatest hits. There was the perfectly roasted chicken, Hungarian goulash, stuffed cabbage, pot roast, and veal cutlets. Sunday was steak night. On my birthday, my mom made me lamb chops. The lamb chops were my favorite.

Here, you have to understand that we never just had one great hit for dinner. There was at least two and sometimes three hits at the same meal. That was because there always were leftovers from a night or two before.

Even the vegetables got to me. My mom would make spinach, mixed in with rice. On top, she would put a perfectly fried egg, and its yolk would break and dribble over the spinach. You have to picture in your mind the crunch of the egg white, the silky yolk intermixing with the spinach, and the tender soft rice that intermingled with every bite.

A large plate of desert would then be set neatly on the table. We always had always cut up fruit, and my mom's world famous apple strudel sitting next to my mom's even more famous rugelach. Rugelach are these rolled up cookies with chopped nuts, cinnamon, and sugar, and a hit of almond flavoring. They were absolute heaven.

At some point at every meal, I would get so full that I did not think I could eat another bite. My mom would turn on the guilt: "Why did I make so much if you are not going to eat?" I would always respond, "That is such a good question. But, I do not know the answer." Of course, I then continued to eat.

If I was unable to finish the food on plate, another retort my mom would have was, "I paid five dollars for that piece of meat!"

Well, that was two dollars less than the week before, I thought, *so maybe I can get away with not eating the fifth piece of whatever dead animal my mom was serving me.*

Of course, after that, I continued to eat.

My mom would then always have to explain to me the exact same thing that probably every other mothers would say in this situation: "There are millions of starving people in this world!" Apparently, my mom believed that she had the power to feed all these starving people right through my stomach.

I could now write about Jewish guilt. I could write about guilt all day long, but it is a bit off topic. This is a book about crankiness.

Despite this nonstop consumption of food, I was never fat. Ok. Maybe I was a bit pudgy, but that was it. I maintained the slight pudginess around my waist through college. This was despite the fact that the college cafeteria had an "all you can eat" policy that I religiously followed. I could get up and get four servings of fried chicken every Sunday dinner. That was followed by make your own two sundaes, both covered in whipped cream and chocolate sauce.

Late at night, sometime around 10 PM, somebody was always going around the dormitory for a dollar contribution toward a pizza. In late 1970s and early 1980s, in Albany, New York, the drinking age was eighteen, and it was always easy to find a dollar-fifty pitcher of beer somewhere. Sutter's burger, across from the SUNY Albany campus, is still the best burger I have ever had. It was twelve ounces of a pure heaven steer burger covered with cheddar sauce, tons of onions and sautéed mushrooms.

Did you hear that? It was a "steer" burger. It was not a hamburger.

It was not a beef burger. It was not a bison burger. It definitely was not a veggie burger. And, what is an ostrich burger anyway? Is it a burger made out of feathers? A steer burger is a burger on steroids. You utter the words "steer burger", and you mouth cannot help but water. Again, I was in pure burger heaven.

After graduating from college in Albany, I went to law school at the University of Pittsburgh. Upon arrival, I had my introduction to a Pittsburgh institution, the Original Hot Dog Shop, affectionately called the "O'Dog". At the world famous O'Dog Shop, they had the best hot dogs with the countless toppings. They also provided vegetables in the form of their amazing French fries with cheese sauce. It was right across the street from the law school.

There was not much time for exercise, but not much time for eating either. That made the O'Dog Shop the perfect place to meet all the law students' dietary needs. It was just so convenient to get a few dogs and a basket of O'Fries from just across the street, munch them quickly down, and get back to our studies. Practically everyone who went to the law school lived on the same diet of hot dogs and fries.

I started practicing law at a small law firm in Pittsburgh after graduating, and here is where it all really started going downhill. I got an addiction to the triple-decker pastrami and chopped liver sandwiches served at a famous grease joint called Fast Ernie's. I was a frequent customer of a pizza place that sold one slice of pizza and half a meatball sub completely covered in mozzarella cheese for three dollars. The restaurant behind the courthouse had amazing meatloaf and gravy that went down really well with an icy cold Iron City beer. On Thursdays, the senior partner of the firm took us out to the North Side to a Greek Orthodox Church for lunch, and we all had the half a roast chicken, a pile of mashed potatoes with gravy, and baklava. Pittsburgh, by the way, is a city that believes in its gravy.

With all these meals, there was always Diet Coke—because, of course, we were watching our figures.

I did not have to worry about law school, and all of a sudden,

I now had time to cook dinner, eat and go out at night. Before I went out, I cooked a massive dinner. The first course of dinner was Campbell's French onion soup. I loved all of the Campbell's soups, especially the chunky ones. After I boiled the soup, I poured it in a bowl, and microwaved the soup covered with two slices of Muenster cheese. I got into the habit of frying things like sausage and onions. Fried liver and onions was one of my dietary food groups at home. I had an addiction to fried liver, and had to have that at least once a week. I bought a deep fryer for my continuous failed attempts at Buffalo chicken wings. I practiced everything that I learned from my mother. I especially made it a priority to perfect my mom's signature potato latkes. Of course, by now, I made sure to smother the latkes with sour cream.

Tuesday nights were called "import night" at the Squirrel Hill Café. After my huge dinner of fried foods, you would think that drinking beer would have been enough. It was not. We always got bags of the beer nuts as well as barbeque and onion garlic potato chips to go with the beer. Typically, the beers were those dark caloric porters and triple stouts. I do not think they even offered a light beer, and if offered, we would have refused. We were proud beer drinkers.

Forget about the weekends. Pittsburgh is a big football town, and I was finally able to spend Saturdays and Sundays watching football, eating chips and pizza, and drinking lots of beer.

I graduated law school in June 1986. By December 1987. I had slowly climbed from 195 pounds to 240 pounds. Yes, my girlfriend dumped me, and the added weight had a little to do with it. On New Year's Day, someone stole my brand new car. I had parked the car right in front of my house. That really sucked. A week later, my boss fired me.

Then, a couple of weeks later, I was still suffering with no girlfriend, no car, and no job. My roommate came up with this great idea to try to cheer me up. He treated me to a Three Stooges Midnight Film Festival. Unfortunately, this was not the hot spot to uplift the spirits of a broken down and depressed overweight bachelor. I can only tell you to try to imagine the kinds of people who go to a Three Stooges Midnight Film Festival. I will give you one hint—they all pretty much dress and act like the Three Stooges—both men and women! Picture yourself going to a "Make America Stoogey Again" rally.

Now, if it was a Midnight Zombie Movie festival, that may have been a bit more fun!

It was at this very point I decided I had had enough. Yes. I was never going to attend a Three Stooges Movie Marathon again. But, I also decided that, no matter how tired I was, I was going to the gym at night. I signed up at the local health club, and the trainer put me on a Lifecycle for three minutes at level one. I did not think I was going to make it. I barely lasted a minute doing this low level of exercise.

Tearfully, I gave up pastrami and chopped liver, and my sandwich of choice became a tuna fish sandwich. I stopped eating fried foods. I gave up potato chips. I stopped putting sugar into my coffee. I was determined to cut out every empty calorie I could find. By the spring of 1988, with the temperatures rising and my weight dropping, I found out that I was able to run. People were constantly asking me if I had AIDS. I replied that I had never felt better and had just started living a healthier lifestyle.

By June 1988, I hit 155 pounds. Instead of dressing up as Santa Claus, I would come home from Pittsburgh, and my father would call me Gandhi. That is another story.

I went from struggling to complete three minutes on a Lifecycle in 1987 to running the Marine Core Marathon in Washington, DC, in 1989. I have run close to fifty marathons since then.

Now we fast-forward to 2000. By then I was married, and my daughter had turned five years old. I noticed that I was starting to gain a few pounds. I never gave much thought to how I lost all that weight back in 1988. It was not a goal; it just happened by accident.

I started thinking about what I did, and I started writing and thinking about what I could do. I realized that, back in 1988, I changed my "normals." It was not a diet, and it made me realize why diets never work. I had a bunch of normals that got me in the predicament of feeling crappy, and if I took a break from those normals to follow a diet, it would only be a short reprieve.

The first change was finding the old normals that may have been healthier than the current unhealthy normals I had been practicing. Old normals are the best ones to start with because they are familiar. There were no goals except for changing my normals. Starting with my old normals, I was able to discover new ones. I started with walking before I tried to run.

We all go through our lives with many normals, through many different times. I noticed that the first change, at least in reference to eating, the abandonment of those unhealthy normals, and go back to healthier but still familiar normals, was the easiest to do. I grew up with my mother making me tuna fish sandwiches for lunch. There were always jars of pickled herring in the refrigerator. Hence, I created the pickled herring diet. If I had a craving for ice cream, I ate a piece of pickled herring. The craving was gone!

With my five-year-old daughter, I noticed that I had become a garbage can. She did not finish her chicken nuggets or fish sticks. No problem—I ate them. What happened if I made one peanut butter and jelly sandwich too many? Not a problem—I can take care of that too. I always had the pizza and birthday cake while serving as a chaperon for my daughter's attendance at friend's birthday parties.

As I realized that this is what I had accomplished twelve years earlier, it was clear what I had to do in 2000. I stopped being the garbage can and let the actual garbage can be the garbage can. I picked a couple of other things that I could do, and I dropped fifteen pounds in three months. While it began as a concept for just losing weight, the concept of stopping and examining my normals became something I found that I could apply to every aspect of my life.

The saying goes, "Crazy is doing the exact same thing over and over again and expecting a different result." It is so true. Imagine that it is the now beginning of spring. Decide that it is time to do some spring-cleaning. It is time to start planting the seeds for the fall harvest.

Examine all of your normals. Think of some of the healthy normals that you may have had many years ago, and lost touch with them in the same way you have lost touch with old friends. Invite them back. Think about new normals that you can take on in the same way you meet and begin a relationship with new friends. Decide what you want to start growing this year. What will be your life changer? Please remember. You only have to walk before you run.

November 2019

CHAPTER 9

CRANKATSURIS MADNESS

I was doing a seminar on negotiation a number of years ago with a group of defense lawyers, and I would like to share with you the hypothetical assignment I gave to them that was going to be the main part of our discussion. Rather than using a legal factual scenario, I decided that I would use a hypothetical scenario that everyone had experience dealing with as part of his or her daily legal practice. Thus, I suggested that since everyone was familiar with the handling of such an issue, it should be no problem for any of them to work out the issue raised.

> Imagine you are in a relationship—or maybe you are in a relationship, but think about your relationship with another person, preferably a spouse, girlfriend, or boyfriend. This person, who we will refer to as "your partner," is mad at you for whatever you did or did not do. We do not need to get into any specifics as to what this person is mad about, just that this person is mad at you.

You happen to be a top-notch defense lawyer. Because your partner has raised a complaint against you, you are given the task of negotiating a resolution to the madness you have been accused of creating.

However, because you are all defense lawyers, you can only raise defenses on behalf of yourself as part of your negotiation through finishing the statement "You should not be mad at me because." These defenses should be similar to the same kind of defenses that you would normally raise every day in your defense practice.

You should also know one more thing about the legal system imposed on you in this relationship: there is a presumption of guilt. In other words, you are guilty until proven innocent.

Here are the responses I received:

- "You are mad at me? I am the one who should be mad at you!" (a counterclaim)
- "I have good reasons why I did what I did!" (affirmative defense; note that in the legal system imposed here, there is a presumption that "good reasons" are always "bad excuses")
- "Sure, I messed up. But I have done lots of other good things!" (offset to any damages caused)
- "I messed up, but you knew I was going to mess up!" (assumption of the risk)
- "I messed up, but I didn't understand what I was supposed to do in the first place!" (no contract because no meeting of the minds)
- "I messed up, but you mess up too!" (comparative negligence)
- "I messed up, but I will fix it!" (mitigation of damages)

I asked the group of defense lawyers this question: Is there was anybody in the room who felt that the strategy - of using the same legal defenses that they used in their everyday practice - was a successful way of ending the madness. They were all honest in their reply that they did not think so. In fact, they felt that this strategy just made the situation worse. They were right.

This particular brand of CrankaTsuris does not dissipate because of whatever defenses that are raised. The person who happens to be mad is not feeling that way because he or she had a previously unrelenting belief that you, in fact, were a perfect human being; they are not looking for reassurance that your perfection has remained intact. Phew—thank goodness for that!

We create our CrankaTsuris typically through our own emotions. This happens more often than the particular CrankaTsuris that is created through what we would considered to be facts. Through our emotional side, we all want to have the experience of being not only heard, but understood as well. If the response is argumentative, judgmental, or a denial of your partner's feelings, the response could be described as "ear-shutting behavior."

Here are some of these types of responses:

A judgmental statement is "That's just stupid."

A dismissive statement is "How can you even get upset by that?" Smirks, grimaces, waves (the "Dr. Phil" mannerisms), and any conduct that is perceived as arrogant act as a response that implies "Well everyone knows that!"

Getting back to these excellent defense lawyers spouting out their excellent defenses reminds me of a saying that lawyers actually like to use. "We have to fight fire with fire!" Whoever came up with that saying probably never worked for their local fire department. I have never seen a fire fighter rush up to a burning building with a tank of gasoline and some matches. They actually used this liquid. We call this liquid: water.

As with any CrankaTsuris, we have to use some water. A CrankaTsuris fire does not put out a CrankaTsuris fire. We need to give the person suffering from the CrankaTsuris the feeling that you actually heard this suffering. Make this person feel very important. Tell your partner what you heard. Ask your partner if you heard correctly. Tell that person what you understand. Also, if you had a misstep, indicate how much you appreciate the feedback.

Once everyone is calm, you could then ask for permission to say something. It should always be forward-looking, to when this situation might happen again. Tell them what would be helpful for you the next time this happens. You can then ask your partner if this suggestion works for him or her as well.

Both of you can now take a deep breath. You and your partner both deserve a hug. You have now successfully ended the madness.

10

A CRANKATSURIS MEDITATION

In *The Last Surviving Dinosaur: The TyrantoCrankaTsuris*, the word "tsuris" is described not to mean those minor daily inconveniences but rather major, life-changing, traumatic events that have brought on suffering that has never been experienced by anyone else since the beginning of time.

However, the truth for most people, when they talk about their tsuris, is that it really is about those minor daily inconveniences. I know how I can be when it comes to this. I find that sometimes the world is burning, and I can be just fine. I just returned from a restful vacation, and I just am able to handle a bit more. Here, a world on flames just does not affect me. At other times, I find that I just have a very low threshold: "Do you really have to make that cud-chewing sound when you are chewing gum?" "If you blow one more bubble, it will be a bubble over your head!" "Can you believe our neighbor? Who in the world mows the lawn in the summer time?"

We all have the experience that it is not always the big stuff that gets to us, but it will be the little things that start to add up. It is the feeling you get when you come home from a picnic on a hot humid day, and you notice that you have hundreds of little mosquito bites.

We are always thinking that we have it the worst. "I would be doing cartwheels if I had your tsuris!"

Imagine having that (someone else's tsuris) as your lifelong dream. You do not want to win the lottery. You do not want the promotion. You do not care about admission to a fine university, get on the basketball team, or have a family, or anything else; your dream is only to have another person's tsuris. Now you have that. You do cartwheels, and you tell the world you finally made it!

The truth is that, if you think it is so hard being you, then, try to be someone else. It is not so easy. At least, you have some experience being you.

My favorite cartoon growing up was *The Flintstones*, and this very concept was the storyline in one memorable episode. Fred and Barney come home, tired from work. Wilma and Betty are exhausted at home. They all complain how life would be a piece of cake if they just switched places.

So they switch. Fred and Barney take care of Pebbles and Bam Bam, and Wilma and Betty go off to the quarry. It turns out that Fred and Barney get a bit too much Bam Bam to handle. Wilma and Betty do just fine at the quarry. Of course, they did. Even then, we all knew that *The Flintstones* was way ahead of its time.

Now we can get back to real tsuris. When we begin to feel overwhelmed by our many minor daily inconveniences, we should sit on a chair in a quiet place or on a cushion and have a CrankaTsuris meditation. Now, meditation can be tricky. I began meditating when I lived in New York and would go to the Village Zendo. We would have summer and end-of-year retreats, where we would spend a week in silence.

We would sit on a cushion from five-thirty in the morning to nine at night, with a few breaks in between. Every meditation experience was different. Some were loud, many quiet. Some terrified me, as if the floor was swallowing me up from beneath. Others were completely blissful. The instructions were very direct. Simply allow the experience to be what it is.

In a CrankaTsuris meditation, with eyes wide open, sit and just breathe in the CrankaTsuris you had that day. Do not judge it. Treat it with compassion. You had an angry feeling, a helpless feeling, a cranky feeling, frustration—whatever it was, just embrace it as true. Do not fight it. Treat it as part of you because that is what it is. Enjoy the feeling of compassion for all this schmutz inside of you, and enjoy the feeling that in your quiet place, it is all safe. No one will judge you. No one will fight back. No one will misunderstand you. It is all safe—just you, with the feelings, compassion, and quiet. Breathe in, and exhale. Let it all out. Get back to the present, and notice the quiet and the space for a few minutes. Exhale.

Start thinking about a CrankaTsuris that you created over a month, year, or lifetime ago. Feel the compassion for all of this as well. Feel safe sitting with this in the quiet space. Again, breathe in, and exhale. Become quiet. Embrace the quiet. Breathe in, and exhale.

Next, what does a CrankaTsuris of a friend, partner, parent, or colleague look like? Breathe that in. Feel compassion for this too. Think about how safe it is for this person to have this CrankaTsuris.

Now, go back to your first CrankaTsuris: those minor daily inconveniences. Check in, and see if they feel a bit softer. Be generous, and feel as much compassion as you did before. Breathe in gratitude. Exhale gratitude. Close your eyes. Sit for five more minutes in quiet.

Ring the bell. Breathe, stretch, and feel the CrankaTsuris cleanse.

CRANKATSURIS BULLY BUDDY PROTECTION BRIGADE

In *The Last Surviving Dinosaur: The TyrantoCrankaTsuris*, our hero, the TyrantoCrankaTsuris, gets laughed at, is ridiculed, and gets bullied by three bigger dinosaurs and does not fare too well with an alligator. Ultimately, she used her own voice, and with the help of the TyrantoKvetchaTsuris, they both cranked and kvetched happily ever after.

Back in those days, there was no computers and no cyberbullying. When I grew up, we did not have computers either. However, of course, kids bullied us, and we did some bullying of our own.

When I was in first grade (and throughout my youth), I had bad allergies. When hay fever season came, I was miserable. My nose was really stuffed. Because of this stuffy nose, I ended up with tons of boogers in my nose. I could have blown my nose in the handkerchief that my mom gave me, but that was not possible. You see, the problem was that she liked to put perfume in all my handkerchiefs. I could not take the smell. It actually made all my clothes smell like women's perfume. It also turned out that making a first grader's clothes smell like perfume was the perfect setup for bullying.

What did I do? I did what any other kid would do: I picked the boogers out of my nose. All the kids did this. Even girls picked their nose! We did not have iPhones to take pictures back then so you have to believe me on this one.

The problems started for me when one of the kids in my class falsely accused me of eating my boogers. This boogie picking kid got all the other kids in the class to call me "boogie man." Thinking back on this time in my life, maybe, this was a little better than being called "perfume boy". Nevertheless, I did not even know what a boogieman was, and it terrified me. Almost immediately, after I gained this name, I saw the movie *The Fly*, when a man turned into a fly; all I could think about was that I was going to turn into a giant booger!

In seventh grade, I admit I did some bullying of my own. I had been going to a Jewish private school, and because it was a Jewish school in the South Bronx, my class ended up having only six kids. I complained about not having many friends because there were only six kids in the class. My parents heard my complaint. That year, my parents took me out of that school and put me into public school. In a new school, and with no friends, I was the prime target for the most annoying kid in the class.

Everyone in the class knew how annoying this kid was and knew to stay away from him. Because of this, this kid had no friends. He was desperately in search of his first friend. Because I was new at the school, I did not know any better to stay away. I was over-eager to make hopefully cool new friends. This was a recipe for new friend disaster.

He immediately announced that not only was he going to be my friend, he was going to be my best friend. I was quite happy for the first two minutes. Then, he quickly began to suffocate me. He just glued on, and I just could not get away from him. He was like a piece of gum stuck in my hair. He was a pimple that I would squeeze, and it would just get bigger and bigger. He had that annoying voice, and he never stopped talking. He would say repeatedly and over again that, I was his best friend in the entire world. He reminded me of that every single day. "Hello, best friend!"

I realized at the age of twelve that you can actually have a Siamese twin just attach to you. No matter what I said, this kid would not get away from me. Finally, I beat him up. I thought that would work—but even that failed. He liked getting beat up. Eventually, I gave up. I was stuck with him as my best friend until high school.

In high school, I joined a bowling league. My bowling ball was my most prized possession. I loved my ball more than anything. In addition, like everyone else's balls, I had my initials engraved on it: "SNJ." It takes only one kid to start something, but one kid started calling me "Snidge." I understand that there are some cool nicknames, and Snidge was not one of them.

The name "Snidge" really bothered me more than anything else did, and back then, nobody cared about name-calling. My parents would say, "Sticks and stones may break your bones, but names will never hurt you!" But, to me, this was way worse than sticks and stones. I did not want to go through high school being "Snidge." I constantly warned people that they should not call me Snidge. If they did, it would be at their own risk. That particular summer, I was working at a sweater warehouse. A fellow worker did not heed my warning, and he paid the price. I dumped a bucket of dirty and sticky, diluted packing glue water on his head. Nobody ever called me Snidge again.

Of course, the teachers did not focus on name-calling and that kind of bullying. After being called a name, I had one teacher ask, "Are you over your feelings yet?"

Back then, some teachers even encouraged bullying. In fifth grade, I ate something that made me gassy. Exactly at two o'clock in the afternoon, I farted. It was a very loud fart. I did not mean to do it. It just happened. Everyone in the class laughed. My teacher made it worse. He made me stand up in front of the class. I had to promise to the class that I would never fart again. I was humiliated. I spent the rest of the year making fart noises when they walked by me.

These days we have cyberbullying, and teachers thankfully are not asking whether the kids are over their feelings. However, what generally happens is that someone reports the cyberbullying to the school, and the whole situation ends up with the adults. The school pulls the bully out of class. The bully ends up with a severe punishment. The bullied student may get counseling. The problem is that, most often, this child can still feel left alone.

What strikes me is how communities come together when acts of violence is targeted against one part of the community. If one group of faith is hurt, all the other groups, whether those with a different faith or no particular faith, give their support. The message is that we are stronger together and this act of violence will not tear us apart.

We can all stop cyberbullying in schools in the same way. The only difference is that we need to work to get the kids to come together before it happens. By the way, it is not such a bad idea for the adults, either.

Instead of a top-down approach, the focus should be working from the bottom up. Each student can have four other classmates, two friends and two non-friends, for a group of five. We form a CrankaTsuris Bully Buddy Protection Brigade. If an incident of cyberbullying occurs against one, the five band together and pronounce that there was an incident. This group is then saying, "We are together and strong, and we support each other." The other brigades also can reach out for support.

This creates community and a feeling of empowerment. Even the kid, who has not been a cyberbully yet, but may be tempted to become one, feels the pull of his or her own CrankaTsuris Bully Buddy Protection Brigade. Because this student has a community for protection against cyberbullying, it may give him or her pause before bullying.

At the end of the school year, when the class has gone a whole year without bullying, the class can reward itself with a big party. The community as a whole comes together to celebrate. Of course, in all good fun, the class can let out a CrankaTsuris; after all, people do get on each other's nerves even occasionally.

12

GET OFF MY BACK CRANKATSURIS

"Get off My Back" CrankaTsuris is one of the most painful types of CrankaTsuris. Your parents are on your back. Your siblings are on your back. Your teachers are on your back. Your boss is on your back. Even your pets can be on your back! You get one person off your back, and another three people jump right on. They are like bugs, and they are always multiplying.

The person handing out the CrankaTsuris is not having much fun either. These people know they sound like a broken record, but they keep trying, hoping that after one thousand tries, the ears on the receiving end will miraculously open up. Both people involved are trying to exert their power over the other, and both end up feeling powerless. There may be guilt on both sides for being unable to satisfy the other. There is a lot of frustration, and feelings are hurt. Nerves are shredded, and relationships become frayed.

This chapter will discuss how you can minimize or eliminate Get off My Back CrankaTsuris. However, before I talk about this, I have to tell a story about me growing up, which ultimately provides the key to unlocking this problem.

Like many other families, we looked forward to watching television when the Olympics came around every four years. The whole family was glued to the television set. Whenever there was a performance that was special, my parents would give me their special commentary.

In 1976 at the Summer Olympics in Montreal, Nadia Comăneci, a Romanian, was the first gymnast awarded a perfect score of 10.0 at the Olympic Games. She was a crowd favorite. The commentators were in awe. Because of her, my father, who was a native of Romania, watched every gymnastics competition that year. After witnessing this amazing performance, his comment to me was, "Why can't you do gymnastics like that?"

Torvill and Dean, brilliant British ice dancers, were in the 1984 Winter Olympics in Sarajevo. They were electric. The crowd loved them. The commentators described their performance as one for the ages. It was something that they had never seen before. Can you guess what was my parents' comment? "Why can't you skate like that?"

Of course, it did not matter that, growing up in the Bronx, I was not taking skating lessons or gymnastics classes. In fact, I skated only once—and very badly—and I never did any gymnastics. Regardless, in my parents' mind, that little piece of reality did not matter. I should have been winning gold medals in ice-skating in the winter and gymnastics in the summer, just like all the other kids in the neighborhood. They also had the firmly held belief that I should be playing concertos on the piano. It did not make a difference that we did not own a piano. I should also spend my time studying to be the world's greatest surgeon who, one day, would find the cure for cancer.

By the way, we also watched *Lifestyles of the Rich and Famous*. I will only say one word about this: Liberace.

I do not fault my parents for having these expectations. It was to be expected. This was because we were too poor to take a beach vacation. Instead, my parents, like everyone else in the neighborhood, went to the back of the apartment building to sit on a bench. They took a "bench" vacation.

Once seated on the bench, all the parents would announce their child's accomplishments. If they had no accomplishments to announce, they would just make some up. It made no difference how big the accomplishment was. It was a silent rule between the parents on the bench that no other parent could question another parent, no matter how outrageous or unbelievable the accomplishment may have sounded. If a parent said that NASA selected their child to be the first person to go to Mars, it had to be true. Everything said was believed, and never questioned. Of course, one by one, they all had to outdo the other. After the bench meetings, my parents went up to give us the report. All the other kids received their acceptance letters to attend fabulous schools. They all got in with a full scholarship. My parents jabbed us with the wonderful jobs the neighborhood kids had all landed.

Then, the punchline came. My parents could not understand how I did not get into the same fabulous schools and land the same wonderful jobs. My parents gave me every opportunity, and I had failed them. They both asked me the question; "When will you give us some nachas?" For those who do not know, "nachas" is the Yiddish word for parental pride.

It made me wish we all lived in Nepal at the foot of Mount Everest. The parents in the nearby village probably had the following conversation, while sitting on the bench, of course.

"So, Sophie, how is your son doing?"

"He is a Sherpa," Esther replied. "And your son?"

"He is a Sherpa too," Sophie said.

Esther then turned to Ruthie. "And what is your son up to?"

Ruthie exclaimed proudly, "He is a Sherpa too, but he also wrote a major concerto that will be performed in Carnegie Hall by the New York Philharmonic. I tell you, I can't stop kvelling!"

There is always one in the crowd.

The point of telling this story is that there will always be many unrealistic expectations out there. People should focus on realistic expectations.

What are they? Both parties should figure this out. They should both get to express what their realistic expectations are for themselves, and what they are for each other.

Parents will love this. My child should have a realistic expectation that I will provide food, clothing, and shelter. The child will write, "I have a realistic expectation that my parents will provide food, clothing, and shelter." Here, there is a match.

Now, it is important that the child should know the realistic expectations that his or her parents should have for them. They could say this: "there should be no expectations of me because my existence on this planet is enough, and by the way, the only realistic expectation for me is that I will play computer games on my iPhone."

That *could* happen. However, the rule should always be that we provide for each other. We help each other. We are a team. The stated purpose is to stop the destructive cycle of the Get off My Back CrankaTsuris. Both sides have to give a bit.

Here is another great example: A child may say, "I have a realistic expectation to be treated like an adult." The parent may then say, "I have a realistic expectation that you will act like an adult. After you meet this realistic expectation, I will have the realistic expectation that I will treat you like an adult."

Now, while that is a perfect example, it may sound a bit too smart and not be taken the right way. To turn this around we could say, "I want you to have a realistic expectation that you will be treated like an adult. I am happy that this is an expectation of yours. I have to be clear on what my realistic expectations are so that this expectation can be met."

The objectives here are both honesty and understanding. We are showing what we are each saying to the other.

It is also important to acknowledge appreciation when a family member shows that they have met the realistic expectations established. "I have a realistic expectation that you will _____, and you have been great. I appreciate that you have met that expectation." That should go both ways. The other person should be happy that first, an important person has expectations of them, and second, those expectations are reasonable.

What you may also find is that one person may try to bargain: "I do not have a realistic expectation that I will be given a trip, car, or fancy dress. But if I do something or work toward something that may be beyond whatever you have a realistic expectation of me doing, could I then change my reasonable expectation of what I can expect in return?"

The answer could be affirmative. Let us try to go beyond our reasonable expectations on both sides.

The point of this exercise is that each side is being honest as to what they see as their own role and how they see the other role. You may agree or you may not. Do not fight over it. If the person you are working through this with cannot meet the expectations that you see as reasonable, you can then ask that person the question, "what can be done to make it easier?" Ask if they can try, and say it is okay to fail because just the effort of trying matters. Say how much you would respect them if they tried and failed.

Plan on a way to go forward. Now that you have laid out the "reasonable expectations", make sure you agree to check in gently every so often to see how the other family member is doing. Check to see whether you need to make any adjustments. Once the family members have all signed on to the program and have practiced this successfully a few times, you have succeeded in getting rid of the Get off My Back CrankaTsuris.

13

WAKE-UP CALL CRANKATSURIS/ CRANKATSURIS SCREW-UP

"Sir, would you like to have a wake-up call?"

There is nobody who actually likes getting wake-up calls. You would never say that you are sleeping in until noon and then tell the hotel concierge, "Why don't you give me a ring sometime around dinnertime, or maybe call a bit earlier so I can catch a bit of happy hour? I always look forward to the wake-up call because it is the best part of my day.

"In fact, the only reason I am staying in your fabulous establishment is because I really love the way you folks do the wake-up call. The phone rings loud, and the best part is that, even after you call the first time, you call me again just to make sure I got out of bed! It is the best!"

Seriously, getting a wake-up call is one of the most painful experiences. You never get the call when you have had the right amount of sleep. You only get the call when you get too little. Of course, the call is always is made at the very point that you are in the deepest part of your sleep cycle. Unfortunately, we ask for a wake-up call because it is the only way that we are able to regain consciousness.

The wake-up call is all about catching an early flight home. It is actually way less painful to stay up all night and leave for the airport on no sleep at all than go to bed for a few hours, with the feeling of a cast-iron frying pan hitting your head when the telephone starts to ring.

A wake-up call can also be that very traumatic event that puts you in such a state of shock that it becomes obvious you have to make a change in your life.

Yes, I had my own real-life wake-up call back in December 1987 and January 1988, when I lost my girl, my car, and my job. I wasn't going to last on a diet of triple-decker sandwiches with pastrami and chopped liver, meatball subs with cheese, lots of pizza, chips, and beer. Maybe two of me would last, but I was determined to return to the size of a single human.

The world itself is in constant need for wake-up calls. I think it is because there are so many things that sends us the message that we all need to wake up. People cannot choose which one to wake up to, and it is just easier to go right back to sleep. Maybe, if we had a worldwide pandemic, people would finally wake up. Unfortunately, we have learned that, even with a pandemic, we see that it does seem very hard to wake up sometimes.

Think of the most obvious example of sleeping through a wake-up call: A hurricane hits the shore with a devastating force and destroys all the homes in its path. People are interviewed on TV talking about how they lost everything they have, and they are even considering moving away from the coast, since this was the fifth and worst hurricane they lived through.

Well, you know what happens. A month goes by, and everyone goes back. They start rebuilding. Maybe, the building will go up a bit higher this time. Of course, it had been a bit higher last time too.

People have very short memories. They have a hard time waking up to accept that changes are required.

The state of crankiness can be a state from which you never really wake up. You get used to that state. You are cranky. Your friends are cranky. Relatives are cranky. You get on the train, and cranky people surround you. Your coworkers are cranky. You come home to turn on the television to a lot more crankiness. Imagine that it is like the house that a hurricane hits and shreds it to pieces: you still just go back and start the next day in the exact same way.

The CrankaTsuris Method is all about waking up to our crankiness and having some play with it, making it just a bit softer. Since nobody is immune to crankiness, we might as well try to learn to have some fun with it.

We all know that every day brings us so many things that ends up making us all cranky. Imagine if you started writing a cranky journal. You could keep a record of each day's cranky moments. There are many things, you can write down, which are universal to everyone's experience. Example: The train was late, and then, I had to stand in a packed subway car. Well, the train was late for many people. You were on the train packed together with everyone else. Remember that you were not alone.

We have many cranky moments that are personal, particularly when it comes to our friends and family. Write those down, and see if there is a repetitive pattern there. You are dealing with the same stuff, repeatedly, and you tell yourself that it may be getting worse.

One of two things typically happens, and neither one is helpful: either you keep it hidden inside yourself, or you lash out in anger with a huge CrankaTsuris. Neither choice is grounding. There is just a bunch of resentment and anger building over time—not much fun.

Do you know what this really is? Crankiness without doing anything about it is actually the first kind of wake-up call we all cannot stand. It is a wake-up call at three o'clock in the morning. You were out late last night. You have a plane to catch. You are exhausted.

You have to quickly pack your bag, make some coffee, take a shower, and get out of the room. Meanwhile, you have that wonderful feeling that a cast-iron frying pan just hit you over the head.

The CrankaTsuris Method is about doing the second kind of wake-up call, where we actually make a change. We slow it down. We give ourselves permission to be heard in a safe and meaningful way. We listen to our loved one's cranky experience.

This is about practicing what is one of my favorite terms: "skillful means." By slowing it down, you can look at things from both a "micro" level, being yourself, and a "macro" level, being the world around you. Everyone starts out saying we are all cranky. I make you cranky, and you make me cranky. Do you know what else is true? If I replaced you with myself, and you replaced you with yourself, you know what would happen. Instead of making each other cranky, we would just make ourselves cranky.

The CrankaTsuris is that little oogie stuck in your throat. Instead of always having it stuck, you play with your friends and loved ones to let it out, and you give permission for them to do the same. It gives us a chance to inhale and exhale air that is a bit cleaner and a lot less schmutzy.

Imagine this is the CrankaTsuris practice when the wake-up call is much later. You get to sleep in not a bit, but a whole lot. You can take your time to get dressed and go downstairs. Happy hour will be waiting for you. Remember that you still get a wake-up call, but this wake-up call is the one that you will enjoy getting up for. This is you trading in survival for transformation.

Part 2. CrankaTsuris Screw-Up.

While we are on the topic of wake up calls and transformation, I want to share something a friend recently posted on social media the following question:

"Instead of using the word mistake, what else can we call it?

A lesson?

A funny story?

A chapter in a book?

An opportunity to practice solving skills?

The important thing is to figure out how it is a gift. Because if you view it as a gift, it will become one."

Now, I am completely on board with this. Then, I read all the responses people wrote in:

"An experience which is one of many that makes you the person that you are."

"A learning opportunity."

"A lesson."

"Opportunity for growth."

"A small glitch."

I was reading the responses, and I was a bit troubled by this. I have no problem with trying to turn the mistake into a positive growth experience. How wonderful! Yet, I was troubled by the feeling that when we focus so much on the positive, and forget the negative, it starts to feel like we lose the opportunity for growth for ourselves with the mistakes that we make. It has both a dismissive and numbing feel to it. "We all make mistakes. Forget about it and move on. Don't dwell on your mistakes." Of course, we move on. By then, there is no growth.

We cannot allow ourselves to move quickly to the positive growth piece of a mistake. We actually have to sit with the mistake. We have to examine the mistake.

I have tried many times over to think of the positive growth I have achieved with every mistake. Unfortunately, I have also been guilty of softening the mistake with that comforting thought of "we all make mistakes" and "don't get so angry with yourself." Guess what happens. I end up making the same mistake many times over again. I tell myself, "I just cannot believe it. How did I make that mistake again?" I passed on the chance for some positive growth.

Some of these mistakes are huge. We all know someone, or we have been that someone, who was in a bad relationship. You hear the story ad nauseam, about how the relationship was this huge mistake, and how this person could not believe he or she was so blind not to see it. A month later, that person ends up in another bad relationship. The new relationship is identical to the bad relationship that this person was amazed how blind he or she was not able to see the first time around.

By repeating our mistakes, we only recreate the exact kind of a world that we do not want to live in.

Once again, we had tried to be kind and comfort the person by saying that we all have made mistakes. We tell the person that it was a learning opportunity, and this should be a chance for positive growth.

Apparently, all that sweet talk sunk in. We made the mistake so okay that it became okay to repeat the mistake. There was no learning from the mistake. There was no growth. There was just continued blindness.

In my reply to this social media question, I wrote that instead of using the word "mistake," I suggested "screw-up." "You really screwed up big time, Steve!"

The screw-up has to feel so big that it becomes a huge CrankaTsuris. Feel it come out at the top of your lungs. Let it out. Sit with the negative part of the screw-up, and imagine that it almost feels like it has you in shackles. For a moment, you may feel imprisoned by it. You may feel enslaved by it. This experience is one that you really need to have.

This does not mean that you have to become obsessed with the mistake. You are not. You acknowledge everything that is in front of you. You use CrankaTsuris as the flashlight and the hi-lighter of the mistake. With your CrankaTsuris, you hold it in your hands for examination, but you do not let it linger. You start the work to have the CrankaTsuris Screw-Up released.

Begin this release. Describe for yourself how would liberation feel? What would freedom from the mistake be like? What would the path to liberation be? Turn your imagination into your new reality.

Only then, can you change the word "screw-up" or "mistake" to real growth and true liberation.

You are now free!

14

CRANKATSURIS LAWYER

There are different kinds of CrankaTsuris. Sometimes, we create a CrankaTsuris by having a bad day. Sometimes, we are in a grumpy mood for no good reason. Sometimes we want something really, really badly and cannot have it. (Alternatively, if we happen to be four years old, we cannot have it and we take it anyway.) The TyrantoCrankaTsuris has arrived!

You then have a little TyrantoCrankaTsuris roaming around your house, and this TyrantoCrankaTsuris must somehow be apprehended, and then, quickly subdued. If you fail in your mission, you may also become a TyrantoCrankaTsuris. Think of *Invasion of the Body Snatchers*—very scary, but I hear it happens!

At this point, you may need a lawyer. You happen to be in luck. I am a lawyer. I negotiate for a living and train others on how to negotiate.

Here, I am the CrankaTsuris Lawyer. I will give the three lessons I give to lawyers to think about when they negotiate as a professional. These lessons are also important when lawyers sense someone pulling them into a negotiation in their personal life. This lesson is even more important for their personal lives when they come face to face with a TyrantoCrankaTsuris.

First, you may find this hard to believe, but the most important rule of negotiation is to avoid arguing. Do not argue! This is counterintuitive for lawyers because they love to argue.

The problem here is if you have your argument and the person, you are arguing with, has their argument, you both end up entrenched in your own positions. Ninety-nine percent of the time, your adversary expected this argument. They saw it coming. Because they heard exactly what they expected to hear, it does not give your argument any real value. You just get back the prepared speech that they had prepared in anticipation of this argument. Of course, you prepared a response in response to this response,

Can you see how it does not get anyone anywhere?

When you argue, you give away power. Instead of arguing, present a firm position: "When I have x, I respond with y. I do not do a, b, or c. It is y." It is a macro approach. The micro approach is too exhausting. The macro approach expands the position to include the repetitive nature of your life or professional experience.

Think about this analogy: You are a vegetarian. You are eating a meal with your friend who is a carnivore. He is eating the most amazing burger, and he wants you to take a bite. He tries to argue with you that you should love meat as much as he does because you will get to experience this heavenly burger. However, there is nothing for anyone to have an argument about. You just do not eat meat. It would be quite strange even to have that argument.

This vegetarian does not need to argue because he or she has certain rules to abide by; "I just do y. That's it."

The best way to learn not to argue is to have a good legal system. There is a certain way of doing things, certain laws: "The law says x, and we do y."

A perfect example would be the following: I go to Israel a few times a year with my partner. We are not religious by any means, but her daughter is Haredi and very religious. They have a multitude of rules and ways to do things. This daughter has four kids. Each of the kids are amazingly well behaved—for the most part. Even these well-behaved kids have a CrankaTsuris in them. They are no different from any other kid here in America. There is a difference with how the parents talk to little cranksters when this happens. When they misbehave and become a little TyrantoCrankaTsuris, my partner's daughter will take the misbehaving kid aside and say, "We do not do these things," or "This is not what we do."

Notice the "we" word. She would never say, "You are being bad," or refer to "you" (which is another lesson in negotiation: not demonizing the other side). "You are being bad" is labeling, but in a way, it is also an argument. If I say that you are bad, you can argue that you are not. There may be a reason you did what you did. "He started first!" However, if this is just not something that we do, does it really make a difference who started it?

Moreover, one important thing we try to avoid is turning into a TyrantoCrankaTsuris ourselves. We keep calm when we explain to our little cranksters what we do.

Kids get older, and they want more and more. They want to go out with their friends, get that outfit, buy the newest computer game, or go to that expensive summer camp. You have rules and the family legal system in place, but they still test it: "Now that I am sixteen, does this law even make sense? I heard that the Supreme Court, which, by the way, all my friends have been appointed to, thinks this law should be overturned and is unconstitutional!"

So being rigid may not be the best thing. This is when I discuss rule number two: I never expect to make a deal if I present this deal as being the best for only me. Nobody cares about my personal best deal. I have to state the position as being the best for the other side. However, the other side is obligated to do the same thing.

We hear this all the time: "Dad, can I go to the concert if I finish my homework and clean my room?" Dad agrees that his child can go if he or she finishes their homework and cleans their room. This conversation suggests there already was a family legal system in place, and the negotiation focuses on each other's interests.

There is flexibility in a mutual interest negotiation. However, sometimes you have to be rigid, as shown in the third rule. I was at a settlement conference in a federal court. I was able to feel the hatred in the room, with the opposing parties having much animosity towards each other. Recognizing this, the judge made a statement: "Principles are nice things to have until they get in the way of reason!"

I loved that line and told that to my partner, who, looking at me as if I came from another planet, and she replied; "Without principles, there is no reason!"

Both lines are somewhat flawed when it comes to looking at our own CrankaTsuris. We need to be mindful that, in fact, principles are a nice thing to have *until they get in the way of reality*. Sometimes people hold on tight to their principles, without even given true consideration to actual reason. That can get dangerous because that person may lose sight of reality or stop listening to reason. Reason is exactly the place where the reality usually resides.

The point here is that we should go through life always being mindful to have some flexibility. If it is always "my way or the highway," we will find ourselves getting into trouble and making many enemies.

If we want to be effective with our own CrankaTsuris, we always need to be mindful of reason and be open to the reason of others. It is about having an open mind, and maintaining a presence to have a clear view of reality.

CHAPTER

15

CRANKATSURIS DOCTOR

There are times when you may need to be a CrankaTsuris Lawyer. But clearly, the CrankaTsuris Lawyer cannot be the answer for every problem. When it comes to family well-being, it is more important to learn how to be a CrankaTsuris Doctor.

Think of the common CrankaTsuris being more common than the common cold. Most people get a common cold once or twice a year, but the common CrankaTsuris may be something you get three or four times a day.

There are those beloved family members and friends who will love to brag incessantly that they are very special. The reason for this particular "specialness" is that they never catch a cold.

Imagine the person who tells you that they never have a CrankaTsuris. The response would be, "Yes, that is because you had a very successful lobotomy operation, and by the way, I need to get the name of your doctor because I am thinking of getting the procedure myself!"

Because the common CrankaTsuris is the most common of all ailments that afflict humankind, we must be able to first self-diagnose and then treat the disease. When we come down with the common cold, we take cold medicine, drink some hot tea and maybe some chicken soup, crawl into bed, and make sure there is a full box of tissues nearby—diagnosis and treatment. Nobody ever gets a cold and thinks, "Hmm, maybe it is foot fungus."

It is vitally important that you self-diagnose and treat your own CrankaTsuris as much as you can. The most important thing to remember is that it is the most common ailment that afflicts everyone, so abandon any bad feelings you may have about being afflicted.

It is not enough to go it alone. Think of yourself getting into a relationship, and both you and your partner become certified as physicians specialized in the treatment of CrankaTsuris. You also both specialize in the prevention of the more serious cases of this disease, when the CrankaTsuris goes untreated and the patient transforms into a TyrantoCrankaTsuris. This is an important piece of knowledge to have because if left untreated, the CrankaTsuris disease is very contagious and can spread quickly.

Here is an interaction between the couple, before they received their medical training:

Partner A comes home to Partner B. Partner B begins to let out a CrankaTsuris about all the minor daily inconveniences that ruined the day. Partner A has a partially formed CrankaTsuris also. However, this particular CrankaTsuris did not yet get a chance to form. It is just metastasizing in Partner A's system.

While Partner A wants to be sympathetic to the CrankaTsuris of Partner B, Partner A also takes it in as one long and smelly verbal fart, and says, "I can't believe that you let that thing upset you! You go on yacking away. You should hear yourself talk sometime. It is a bit insane!"

Since you have made it up to this part of the book, you should now realize that this response is not the best and most appropriate treatment for a CrankaTsuris, and it will only make the CrankaTsuris worse. The worse the CrankaTsuris gets, the more contagious it becomes. If this goes on much longer, the couple slowly transforms into a TyrantoCrankaTsuris and a TyrantoKvetchaTsuris, long known to be the most dangerous creatures on the planet.

The good news is that you do not need three years of medical school to obtain your certification for treating CrankaTsuris disease. The first step is to recognize each other's particular kind of CrankaTsuris. Become familiar with it, so that the CrankaTsuris can be both self-diagnosed and diagnosed by your partner.

Once you are both familiar with each other's CrankaTsuris, find out what each other needs when they become afflicted. Write it down. Practice it. You never know when a CrankaTsuris will strike a person.

Most importantly, when your partner has a CrankaTsuris, encourage your partner to let it all out. Think of it in the same way you would think of a cold. You would not tell your partner with a cold and stuffy runny nose, "Whatever you do, do not blow your nose! You have to keep all that good phlegm inside!" So let them blow it all out. If they do, the CrankaTsuris immediately becomes less contagious. Once it becomes less contagious, you as the treating physician can give your partner a great big hug. The hug gets out whatever remains of the CrankaTsuris.

Let me tell you about a recent experience I had. This will give you one more thing to think about, now that you are working toward your CrankaTsuris doctor degree. I was taking care of a good friend, who was not doing well. She thanked me for going over. I replied that it was both my pleasure and joy.

As I said this, I noticed the big difference between the two. Pleasure is something we focus too much on. It may bring a feeling of euphoria, but it is for just that moment. Joy is more intimate and long lasting. The rewards for joy are enormous because of the durability and substance. Think about the huge rewards that await you as you both start playing CrankaTsuris doctor.

CHAPTER 16

BARKING UP THE WRONG TREE CRANKATSURIS

Many years ago, when my daughter was growing up, we were lucky to have this amazing dog. His name was Albus Dumbledog. He must have come from another world because what made him so special was that he was a talking dog.

Yes. I owned a talking dog. We had some amazing conversations. I got to learn so much about dogs. He was also an amazing listener. I would come home from a bad day at work and tell him about all of my problems. When I asked him if it was okay to tell him all my complaints of the day, he would look at me with those understanding eyes, and he would always tell me the same thing:

"You are barking up the right tree, man!"

Unfortunately, I was never able to return the favor in the exact same way.

I would take Albus for long walks and every so often, he would see a squirrel or a cat running up a tree. Albus became excited, and hurriedly, went up to the base of the tree, and started barking. No matter how long he barked, the squirrel or the cat at the top of the tree would not come down. The squirrel was particularly mean, tossing nuts down at poor Albus.

Finally, I had to say:

"You are barking up the wrong tree, dog."

Albus was a very smart dog, and after being told that he was barking up the wrong tree, he went home, and looked up on the internet exactly what type of tree had the best bark. Surely, he thought, if he figured out the type of tree that had the best bark, he then could be barking up the right tree.

After a few minutes of searching, Albus had his answer. It was the Oak tree. Albus became very excited. He heard that on the other side of town next to a pond stood a giant Oak tree. Finally, he thought, he could bark up the right tree.

I took Albus out for a walk the next day, and he made a special request. Albus never had made a special request before so I knew that this must be an important request.

"Papa. When you take me for a walk, can you take me by the giant Oak tree on the other side of town?"

"Why?" I asked. What is so bad about peeing on any other tree in our neighborhood or on a hydrant like you normally do?"

"Papa. I do not want to pee on the Oak tree. I just hear that the Oak tree has this special bark. I just want to see it."

The next morning, I drove Albus to the park that featured this Oak tree. Sure enough, Albus noticed three squirrels and two cats crawling up the Oak tree, and started to bark like crazy. No matter how much Albus barked, the squirrels and the cats would not come down.

Finally, I had to tell Albus:

"You are barking up the wrong tree, dog."

Albus turned to me defiantly and said:

"Papa, I have the right tree. This is the tree with the best bark. I will keep on barking because I know I have the right tree!"

Albus kept barking. He just would not stop. People came from all the ends of the park to watch Albus bark. One person asked me:

"Does he always bark like this?"

I replied; "Yes, but his bark is way worse than his bite."

The person who asked the question took one look at Albus' teeth. He noticed that they were the biggest fangs he ever witnessed on a dog. Terrified, and now knowing that Albus' bark is worse than his bite, this man turned around and ran as fast he could in the opposite direction.

After a few hours of barking, Albus' voice began to get a bit hoarse, and his bark sounded more like a croak. The croak was so effective that hundreds of frogs from the pond nearby jumped out and surrounded Albus. With every croak from Albus, all the frogs danced around and formed a circle around Albus. Albus was delighted with his newly found frog fan club. The squirrels and the cats who had been hiding at the top of the Oak tree came down to join in the fun.

I told Albus, chuckling; "Isn't it interesting. You barked up the wrong tree, but you croaked down the right pond."

This incident reminded me of another story. Our next door neighbors were the Barker family; Woody and Maple Barker and their two kids, Birch and Willow. They were all the kindest and most generous neighbors on the block. If you needed any kind of help, you were sure that you would be able to count on one of the Barkers to pitch in.

However, it was not always this way. In fact, they were the exact opposite. They were the meanest and stingiest people in town.

Apparently, the Barkers developed a severe case of Barking up the Wrong Tree syndrome. If one family member made any request to another, the answer was always the same:

"You are barking up the wrong tree."

If any neighbor asked for help, the answer was always the same.

"You are barking up the wrong tree."

Anyone who would walk by the house would hear the same commotion going on. One family member after another could be heard shouting:

"You are barking up the wrong tree."

Because of all the barking that the Barkers were doing, all of the Barkers lost their voices. All of a sudden, the house went completely silent.

The Barkers were terrified that they had lost their primary way of communication. Immediately, the next day, they paid a visit to their primary physician.

The primary physician shook his head, and told the Barkers, that unfortunately, there was nothing that he can do for them.

He told them:

"You are barking up the wrong tree."

The primary physician did come up with a suggestion.

"I recommend that you go see this family therapist. Her name is Dr. Sylvia Burt. She is a Certified BURT therapist."

"What exactly is a BURT therapist?" Woody croaked.

"A BURT therapist specializes in teaching people how to bark up the right tree, and how to be the right tree to bark up to. She is the best there is."

The Barkers went straight to see Dr. Burt. They practiced for weeks learning how to bark up a right tree, and to be the right tree to bark up to. Once they mastered their newly found barking abilities, all of the Barkers' voices returned.

None of the Barkers ever barked up the wrong tree again.

Of course, our CrankaTsuris is our way of barking. If we find that we are always barking up the wrong tree, the CrankaTsuris gets worse and worse. These simple stories teaches us the power we get when we finally can feel safe to bark up the right tree. This is the true essence of the CrankaTsuris Method.

CRANKATSURIS IN PARADISE

Summertime. School is now out. Finally. It is now that time of the year when the family starts to take off for their long-awaited summer vacation. Before you consider all the things that could go wrong on a vacation, we need to take a look at all the characters typically cast in the lead roles of this CrankaTsuris drama.

First, we have the kids. They are all excited that they get to embark on this great adventure. Little Bobbie and Susie both cannot wait to experience new things. For weeks they have been daydreaming about the trip, and now it is about to happen. They were so excited the night before leaving that they could not go to sleep. On the day of the trip, the parents pull kids out of bed. Of course, this is because of their exhaustion from staying up the night before.

Parent A is the one responsible for the packing list: sunscreen, Tylenol, bug spray, bandages, bathing suits—the list is so long that it is essentially the entire inventory of the whole house. Yes, it is only a week's vacation, but the goal of Parent A is to see if we can pack for an entire year. This parent is so proud of the packing list. This parent also feels resentful that they are the one solely responsible for the list. What makes this even worse is the fact that the rest of the family takes turns criticizing this masterful piece of work that took so much effort.

"Why are we packing so much food? Don't they have restaurants that we can eat at?"

The rest of the family have problems with the list, so instead of discussing the problems, they each make sure to innocently forget a few of the items that they were supposed to pack.

"If I forget to pack my bathing suit, Mom and Dad will just have to buy me a new one! Hooray!"

Parent B is the planner. Parent B is responsible for making travel arrangements; finding the perfect hotels; doing check-ins and reservations; and scheduling events, tours, rides, and dinner reservations. Parent B is also the over-planner, making sure there is absolutely no downtime whatsoever. Parent B is proud of this elaborate plan but also feels resentful that nobody participated in the planning or has even shown the least bit of interest.

The rest of the family have been trained to know that Parent B is the planner, and they want no responsibility in the planning because that frees them up to blame the family planner if anything goes wrong. Parent B knows this, and that adds to this parent's resentment.

One parent is the early person. This parent believes that we have to take into account possible traffic jams, the car breaking down, the airport lines being long, and kids not getting ready on time. This parent wants to leave three hours earlier than may be necessary.

The other parent is always the late person. This parent remembers very well the time the family got to the airport three hours early and had to just sit around, so this parent has taken on the mission of leaving at a time when there is not a moment to spare.

Even, if things go reasonably well, like the bikes don't not fall off the bike rack and crash into the cars behind while speeding down the highway, this situation, if left unchecked, will result in CrankaTsuris in Paradise.

Utilizing the CrankaTsuris Method, this is a solvable problem. This is what you need to do: At least a few weeks before the vacation, schedule a CrankaTsuris party for the whole family. Order a pizza, get some of the kids' favorite foods, and make sure it is a fun setting. Once everyone gets in a good relaxed mood, it will be time to take turns and let out the vacation CrankaTsuris.

Let it all out. Go on and on until it starts getting silly. The secret to a good CrankaTsuris is that it starts out as being very serious, but the longer you go, the sillier it gets. Each CrankaTsuris should end with, "And it makes me feel really, really mad and sad, and I just want to cry!"

In this game, the rest of the family has to come up with ideas on how they can help the family member with their CrankaTsuris. Once that person finishes, the next family member gets to go. Again, the other members have to come up with ideas to help each other out. When everyone is done, it is time to start writing the CrankaTsuris packing list.

Things can still go wrong on vacations, but this exercise is important to wash away any of the resentment before you go. You can pack a car full of clothing, food, and everything else, but nothing will take up more room in the car than resentment. With any vacation, make sure you always travel light when it comes to resentment.

18

THE CRANKATSURIS CHICKEN

Mr. Schlemiel wanted to retire in the country and live on a chicken farm, but he felt that he could never afford it. It was his lifelong dream. He vigilantly checked *Chicken Farm Real Estate Magazine* every week, and the prices were always way above what Mr. Schlemiel could afford.

One day, Mr. Schmegeggi approached him. He had heard about Mr. Schlemiel's dream of owning a chicken farm. He told Mr. Schlemiel that he was in luck. Mr. Schmegeggi had a chicken farm that he was selling for a tenth of the price of the average chicken farm.

Mr. Schlemiel could not believe his luck. "I'll take it!" he exclaimed without thinking.

When Mr. Schlemiel got to the chicken farm, he immediately discovered that there were no chickens. "What kind of a chicken farm has no chickens!" he cried. Being very upset over this, he called Mr. Schmegeggi to complain: "There are no chickens on the chicken farm!" Mr. Schlemiel screamed.

Mr. Schmegeggi thought about this and said, "You can't count your chickens until they hatch."

For a brief second, Mr. Schlemiel thought this made sense. Then he thought it over and got upset yet again. He said to Mr. Schmegeggi, "But there are no chickens to hatch because there are no chickens to lay eggs!"

Mr. Schmegeggi thought about this and said, "Have you bought some eggs? People always ask me "what came first, the chicken or the egg?" I will give you the answer. It is the egg. Because I like you, and also, because I feel a bit guilty, let me tell you what I did for you. I just went to the supermarket, and I bought you two dozen eggs, pastured and cage-free, no less."

Mr. Schlemiel was not happy with this. He snarled back, "I do not want an omelet! I want chickens! This is not acceptable!"

Mr. Schmegeggi saw that this did not help so he pointed out the window and said. "Just open your eyes, and look outside. The chickens crossed the road to get to the other side."

Mr. Schlemiel looked out the window and saw the other side of the road with hundreds of chickens. He noticed that all the grass were greener on the other side. In fact, he also noticed that, on his side of the road, his side was a dust bowl. There was just a few blades of yellow dried up grass covering his entire chicken farm.

Seeing this, Mr. Schlemiel complained, "Look at the grass on my farm, and look at the grass across the road. You never told me that the grass is greener on the other side!"

Mr. Schmegeggi quickly said, "But the grass is always greener on the other side!"

Mr. Schlemiel was fuming. "That's a paltry excuse if I ever heard one!"

Mr. Schmegeggi said, "Of course it is not; it is a poultry excuse."

As Mr. Schmegeggi continued to egg Mr. Schlemiel on, Mr. Schlemiel was in a very fowl mood indeed!

THE CRANKATSURIS SCHLEMIEL

Mr. Schlemiel is a special person because he is one of those people who has gone through his entire life with the experience of lots and lots of tsuris. Yet, amazingly, he had never experienced a CrankaTsuris. The reason for this is quite simple: he spends his entire life letting people take advantage of him. He always thought that was just the way things were; he did not know any better.

One day he woke up and thought to himself; *this is a new day. I will not let people take advantage of me. I am going to find a lawyer, the best lawyer, and I am going to sue those people who tried to take advantage of me. I will show them, and bring them to their knees. Nobody will dare take advantage of me again!*

Mr. Schlemiel found the best lawyer, and the lawyer's name was Mr. Schmegeggi. How did Mr. Schlemiel figure out that Mr. Schmegeggi was the best lawyer? Mr. Schemegeggi told him so. Yes! This same Mr. Schmegeggi was the Schmegeggi who took advantage of Mr. Schlemiel, and sold Mr. Schlemiel the chicken-less chicken farm! You see. Mr. Schlemiel had worked hard his entire life to get the reputation of being a Schlemiel.

Mr. Schmegeggi promised Mr. Schlemiel that when the case was over, nobody would ever mess with Mr. Schlemiel again. With the money he would get, Mr. Schlemiel would live a "tsuris-free" life.

The case proceeded to trial, and Mr. Schlemiel had a good case. We know this, because, Mr. Schlemiel was presented with an offer of five million dollars to settle the case. He was very excited with the news, so excited that he went to Mr. Schmegeggi to tell him he wanted to take the money.

"Mr. Schmegeggi, please let's take the money. This is a lot of money for me, and I do not see five million dollars every day. Let's settle and go home!"

Mr. Schmegeggi shook his head in strong disapproval. He replied, "Mr. Schlemiel. The five million dollars is an insult to my reputation. I will get you many times more than that. We will take the case to trial!"

Mr. Schlemiel responded sheepishly, "OK."

The case then proceeded to trial, and it did not go too well. The jurors looked at Mr. Schlemiel with puzzled expressions and appeared openly hostile whenever Mr. Schmegeggi opened his mouth. Still, the defendants presented a three million dollar settlement offer was to Mr. Schlemiel.

Mr. Schlemiel, hearing this, ran over to Mr. Schmegeggi and said, "Mr. Schmegeggi, please let's take the money. I do not think the jurors like you very much, and they look at me as if I am some kind of schlemiel. I do not see three million dollars every day. Please settle."

Mr. Schmegeggi looked at Mr. Schlemiel and said, "Mr. Schlemiel, trust me—no worries. I am the professional here. I plan to kill the jury with my closing argument!"

Mr. Schlemiel responded sheepishly, "OK."

The closing argument did not go very well. It was clear that by the time they got to the closing argument, all of the jurors had lost interest—they were all fast asleep. Still, the defendants presented a settlement offer of one million dollars to Mr. Schlemiel.

Amazingly, Mr. Schlemiel was able to stay awake during the

closing argument, and he saw what was going on. He ran over to Mr. Schmegeggi, got down on his knees, and begged. "Mr. Schmegeggi, please, let's take the money. You said that your closing would be a killer, but I did not realize that would mean putting them all in a deep coma. I do not see one million dollars every day. Let's take the money!"

Mr. Schmegeggi said; "I have a duty to protect the interests of my client, and the interests of my client is to take the case to verdict!"

Mr. Schlemiel responded sheepishly, "OK."

The jury came back and awarded Mr. Schlemiel nothing, with a verdict in favor of the defense. In fact, because they were upset at Mr. Schmegeggi for forcing them to his listen to his nonsense for two weeks, the jury awarded all of the defendants a million dollars to cover all their legal fees!!

The next day, Mr. Schlemiel picked up the phone and called Mr. Schmegeggi. The receptionist picked up the phone and said, "Oh, Mr. Schlemiel, Mr. Schmegeggi was very upset and distraught over losing your case. He climbed to the top of the tallest building. He jumped off the top of the tallest building. Mr. Schmegeggi is dead."

Mr. Schlemiel responded, "OK."

The next day Mr. Schlemiel again called and asked for Mr. Schmegeggi. The receptionist again answered the phone and explained, "Mr. Schlemiel, like I told you yesterday, Mr. Schmegeggi was very upset and distraught over losing your case. He climbed to the top of the tallest building. Come to think of it. He probably took the elevator. The man was one hundred pounds overweight, and I do not think he could walk up a flight of stairs. Yet, we know this. He went to the top of the tallest building. He jumped off the top of the tallest building. Mr. Schmegeggi is dead."

Mr. Schlemiel responded, "OK."

The next day, again, Mr. Schlemiel picked up the phone and asked to speak to Mr. Schmegeggi. Once again, the receptionist answered and politely explained, "Mr. Schlemiel, like I explained the last two days, Mr. Schmegeggi was very upset and distraught over losing your case. He climbed to the top of the tallest building. He did not take the elevator. The elevator was out of service. Nevertheless, he climbed to the top of the tallest building. He jumped off the top of the tallest building. Mr. Schmegeggi is dead."

Mr. Schlemiel responded, "OK."

For the next week, Mr. Schlemiel continued to call every single day, asking to speak to Mr. Schmegeggi. Finally, Mr. Schmegeggi's partner picked up the phone, exasperated, and said, "Mr. Schlemiel, for the last ten days you have called asking for Mr. Schmegeggi. Every day we tell you the same thing: Mr. Schmegeggi was very upset and distraught over losing your case. He climbed to the top of the tallest building. He jumped off the top of the tallest building. Mr. Schmegeggi is dead! Why do you keep calling?"

Mr. Schlemiel responded, "I like to hear the story."

CHAPTER

20

FACT OR FICTION CRANKATSURIS

People like to say, "You have a right to your opinion, and I have a right to my opinion." However, the problem is that we do not really believe that anymore. What we now believe is this: "You have a right to your opinion, as long as you agree to my facts. Of course, if you agreed to my facts, then it is obvious that you would absolutely share my opinion. Therefore, you only have a right to my opinion. You have no right to your own opinion. Do not worry about coming down with Opinion Deficiency Syndrome because I happen to have lots of strong opinions!"

Because this is now what we truly believe, we shift closer to people who share our opinions, and society becomes more polarized. People start believing in alternate facts and fake news, and they can create their own reality and reject other people's reality. The end-result of this is that we end up with "Fact or Fiction" CrankaTsuris. It is not healthy, and just like other forms of CrankaTsuris, this form of CrankaTsuris needs to be treated.

I, at times, suffer from Fact or Fiction CrankaTsuris. My personal Achilles heel, which many others may share, is my problem with math. I happen to be a believer in math. For some reason, I find myself falling for the bait, and I then get into arguments with people who do not believe in math. They believe in "anti-math" At times, I wish I were an anti-math believer. I believe that if I was an anti-math believer, then I too, would always be convinced that I, alone, possess the truth of all that is good in the world and have all the answers.

If you, and someone who is very important to you, become consistently stuck in Fact or Fiction CrankaTsuris, here is an approach that you can try. This is particular to my background as a trial attorney. Think of what a trial is. There are two sides with contradictory opinions about the facts of a case, and each side wants the jury to believe their opinion and reject the other side's opinion.

We need to have our focus on two particular parts of the trial. It is the beginning and end of the trial that are the opening statement and the closing argument.

The opening statement is the portion of a trial where you present to the jury what you believe the evidence will show. In giving their opening statement, attorneys cannot argue the case. Rather, the rule is this: Judges permit attorneys to state to the jury exactly what they believe the evidence to be. That is it.

Therefore, instead of just talking about this belief on what the evidence will be, we talk about the promises we can make.

"Ladies and gentleman of the jury, I will be making some promises to you now as to what the evidence will be. Moreover, here is an important thing to know and keep in mind: I am not the finder of fact; you folks are. If I keep my promises, I think that you should find for my client. However, do you know what? If I do not keep my promises, I want you to find for the other side. Where can you find a fairer deal than that?"

Think about that for a second when you get into an argument. How many times do you tell the person you are arguing with that they are the finders of fact? This probably does not happen too often. In fact, the opposite is always true.

I go on. "I believe the promises I make to you are airtight, ironclad, and rock solid. I am so confident that I will keep my promises that I am now inviting my opposing counsel to stand up and tell you folks that I will not be keeping my promises."

I can tell you, from experience, that I would only give that particular speech if I were 100% sure that I would keep my promises; a jury will not stand anything less than someone who cannot keep their promises.

Now we can get back to the two people having a Fact or Fiction CrankaTsuris episode. We are convinced in our own beliefs and the facts that they are based upon, and we desperately want the victory of convincing the person who we are arguing with of the exact opposite position that they are taking.

On the other hand, they are busy trying to claim the exact same kind of victory you are seeking. Can both of you say you are the finder of fact? Can you both say, "If I do not keep my promises, I want you to come to the exact opposite conclusion that I have asked you to make"? If you find that you have some difficulty doing this, you are not alone.

Even if you have math on your side, you have to remember that, even here, somebody else will have anti-math.

So, with this, we are still left with argument, and as an attorney, in my closing argument, I would try to tie everything together with one simple statement: "Ladies and gentlemen of the jury, I am so pleased to report to you that this was my favorite case to try. This is my favorite case! It is not because of fancy experts or sexy issues—no, not at all. It is because, with this case, I can rely solely on the common sense of the jury, and whenever I can rely on the common sense of the jury, juries always do the right thing."

The point here is that the jury is hearing two completely different stories. I want to have the story that resonates with the common sense of the jury.

Now, you may read this and feel more emboldened that, in some argument you are having with another person, you can win your case. You can make promises, and you can tie it to principles of common sense. That is fine. However, listen to the other person talking. Start to try to decipher whether they believe as much as you do in their own promises and in their own common sense. They see red; you see blue.

Even better, think of all the times that you have been caught up in an argument and neither person can make those airtight, ironclad, and rock-solid promises; the basis of each person's argument relies solely on what they would like to believe. "I want desperately to believe the world is flat because if it is round, I get so scared that I will just fall off. It can't be true, and I will not believe otherwise."

I can only guess that this is why some brilliant person, probably some genius philosopher, many years ago came up with the rule that "we all have the right to our own opinion."

Yes. We can all just shrug and say that we have a right to our own opinion. But here, instead of seeing only red or blue, we should take a breath, and start to see if there is a little bit green out there. If you have only been seeing blue, just maybe the color is red. If you have only been seeing red, just maybe, the color is in fact blue.

Trust yourself that once you do that, you will not fall off the world that you have planted your feet on. You just get to experience a much bigger world.

21

CRANKATSURIS NINCOMPOOP

Anyone who has worked in an office setting may have likely had been a part of this particular situation:

Everyone has gathered in the big boardroom. At the head of the table sits the President, Vice President, or whomever the company anointed as the decision maker of the day. Detailed presentations are directed specifically to the important decision maker. Arguments for different options on the proper course of action are laid out in precise detail. Finally, when this part of the meeting is completed, everyone looks to the front of room with breathless anticipation on what the decision from the person who makes the big bucks will be.

This person, who probably slept through the presentations, wakes up and speaks.

"My gut tells me that we should probably do Option C."

I have a confession to make. I never fully grasped the decisions that are made solely in the gut. Here is another thing. Whenever someone tells you what his or her gut says, that person never volunteers to tell you what the brain said. What if the brain felt the exact opposite choice was the way to go. It makes perfect sense that we get to hear what the brain is telling the decision maker.

It could be even worse. What if it turns out that the brain is completely silent, and has no thoughts at all. The brain of this important person is no longer in service, and the only working part left is the gut. Typically, we also see that the gut is actually the biggest part of this person's body.

Do want my opinion? This is what I think. The people around the room put their heart and soul and spent days on these thoughtful presentations. This decision maker is being paid the big bucks to make these big decisions. We have a rightful expectation that this brain is in good working condition. We should require that this well-paid brain be put to good use at least half the time.

Fifty percent is not too much to ask.

If the gut is more important that the brain, you would never see, someone brag on their resume that, as part of their qualifications, they can speak five languages fluently. Under this concept, it would be more impressive if the resume stated that the applicant has eaten in five different ethnic restaurants, and make a point of eating Italian at least once a week.

Having an impressive gut may be an important factor if you happen to be applying for the Nathan's Hot Dog Eating Contest, but if you are relying only on what is going on in your gut, the decisions you may be making may be come out of the wrong artifice in your body. I do not know this to be a fact, but I can only guess that the word "nincompoop" was created after watching someone make many bad gut decisions.

Unfortunately, the planet has millions of nincompoops walking around.

Of course, what does many bad gut decisions lead to for many people? It leads to a CrankaTsuris.

"You have guts" on the other hand, does not necessarily mean that you happened to be born with two or more stomachs. This is all about courage, but having courage is about thought and preparation, and having mental toughness.

The best example that come to my mind was Jackie Robinson. Jackie Robinson was the first African American to play Major League baseball. He knew that the path he was about to take would be difficult. He mentally prepared himself. The most important thing that he did was to set an example with abundant grace. He never stooped to the lower level of insults and taunts. This would have been the understandable and easy thing to do. Jackie Robinson had guts.

This comparison of "using your gut" and "having guts" leads me to think a bit about how we make too many judgments these days. The judgments come not from thoughtful retrospection, but from our gut. It is all from emotion. Every day, we find ourselves baited by this constant flood of false narratives and partial narratives. We do not do the mental work needed to ask the right questions. If we end up spending all of our time making judgments only from the emotional perspective, that gut judgment gets overused, and the result is a CrankaTsuris. We create this CrankaTsuris when we get overwhelmed, angry or depressed.

I am certain that someone has told you that he or she cannot watch the news anymore because it is too depressing (and overwhelmed and angry). That is what they say. What this person really is saying is that the news is fueling a CrankaTsuris inside them.

This issue of "judgment" came up for me when I heard on the radio that one of the Boston Marathon bombers had his death sentence overturned by the First Circuit Court of Appeals. I had a reaction and feelings about that. It was personal.

The reason is that I ran the Boston Marathon that year. I started the race in the first wave. My starting position was in the tenth coral of the first wave. This was the last coral. I just barely made the first wave. The second wave started thirty minutes later. If I started the race in the beginning of the second wave, I would have been crossing the finish line exactly when the bombs went off.

I was lucky. Actually, I was very lucky. A year earlier, I ran the

First Jerusalem Marathon. Two days before, I left the place where I was staying to go to the Marathon Expo to pick up my bib number. I was walking with my daughter, Vita, and we made a wrong turn and ended up walking through the Old City.

At the very moment we would have gotten to the Expo, a bomb went off across the street at the Jerusalem Bus Station. Tragically, it killed a few people and injured others.

Getting back to the Boston Marathon, what still lives with me to this day is that when I made the final left turn to head to the finish line at the Boston Marathon, I made a point of giving high fives to all of the kids who had their hands out, waiting to be high fived. I was a kid's hero, running towards the finish line, and he was going to get a high five. Afterwards, I heard that one of those kids had died because he was not lucky.

When I heard that the death sentence of the person, who was responsible for the death of a little kid, was overturned. I had an emotional reaction. Then, on the radio, I listened to all of the people that the news reporter interviewed on this story. The only question that the interviewer asked these people was what they thought about the decision. Of course, it was unanimous. Everyone interviewed felt that it was the wrong decision.

The point here is that, in this case (as in many others), the media was only going for the emotional decision, the one coming out of the gut. Then, I thought that it would have been nice that the report would include the reasoning for that decision so we can have some understanding. We can learn about the basis of the arguments that the attorneys made in opposition, and hear why the Appellate Court disagreed with those arguments.

Once we received this information, we can understand the decision, but still disagree with decision. We can disagree and we can respect the decision. We can even think that, despite the fact that we disagree with the decision, the judges who made the decision had guts.

Let us get back to the person who tells you that he or she cannot watch the news anymore because it gets them depressed. Compare that to an excellent well-made documentary. You will never hear someone complain that he or she can no longer watch well-made documentaries. The reason is because such a documentary feeds and make you use your brain together with your gut.

If the Last Surviving Dinosaur, the TyrantoCrankaTsuris, made many decisions from the gut, it was understandable and expected. The TyrantoCrankaTsuris, like all the other dinosaurs who roamed the earth, had a tiny little brain. Some say that the brain was so small, it was hard to even detect, and completely useless.

We now have learned that all humans evolved from the TyrantoCrankaTsuris, and that is why we all suffer from the common CrankaTsuris. However, lucky for us, our brains are vastly more developed and are much bigger than the TyrantoCrankaTsuris. We should all be mindful to remember to use our brains, and "have some guts" when we use them. By doing so, we can learn to lessen the effects of the CrankaTsuris, and make the world a much happier place.

22

CRANKATSURIS BOREDOM

Do you remember the *Lawrence Welk Show*? If you are less than thirty years of age, or maybe under forty years old, you have probably never heard of the show. However, I am a bit older, and I can tell you a bit about the *Lawrence Welk Show*. It ran for four years locally in Los Angeles, from 1951 to 1955, and then nationally from 1955 to 1971, followed by first run syndication from 1971 to 1982.

Maybe, if you happen to walk in to an assisted living facility, it could be playing on a TV somewhere through a local cable network, most likely on the Assisted Living Channel. If not there, try the Memory Loss Channel, and you will be sure to find it.

Overall, some TV Network genius produced 1,065 episodes of the Lawrence Welk Show. Now, when I learned that particular statistic, it came as a shock to me. We are not talking about a show like MASH, or Seinfeld. It was the Lawrence Welk Show! As a child, I suffered, because my parents forced me to watch the *Lawrence Welk Show* every single week. There must be something written by professionals out there that would consider this to be illegal torture!

Just at the time the show was going to be on, I hid in my room, hoping my parents would forget about me. Of course, this never worked. Five minutes before the show was starting, my father would come into my room and say, "Come sit with the family! The *Lawrence Welk Show* is coming on!"

Yes. I spent the first twelve years of my life watching the *Lawrence Welk Show*. Until now, when I finally learned about the 1,065 episodes, I was always under the impression that I had been watching the exact same episode every week.

Every episode consisted of perfect-looking, grown-up mostly white people with perfect smiles, dressed in matching clothes with bright colors that I can only imagine were designed by Baby Gap, singing and dancing in a way that slowly turned your brain to mush. It was as if some evil genius enemy designed the *Lawrence Welk Show* to be a secret weapon. They would get every American to watch the show, we would all go into a deep trance, and while we were in this comatose state, they could simply walk in and take over.

If you need a better description of this show, just imagine an hour of slow polka music. Just think about the name "polka" and compare it to other genres of music. There is rap, hip-hop, rock and roll, pop, jazz, rhythm and blues. They all sound cool in their own special way.

Then, there is polka. It sounds like something you get when you are sick.

"Mommy! I have a polka in my belly, and it hurts really bad!"

"Oh my! We will have to go to the doctor and have it checked out right away!"

I actually imagined that while I was watching the show. I would study my parents closely just in case they would fall asleep. I would then wake them up so we would be ready for an enemy attack. It was so boring!

Despite the traumatic memories, I look back now at these boring times with fondness and nostalgia. It is, because with iPhones, games, gadgets, and five hundred channels on cable, nobody gets permission anymore to be bored. Our brains need to be stimulated every moment of every day. "Are we there yet? I am bored," is part of the rehearsal practice by every preteen at the Annual National Preteen Convention.

When a child tells a parent that he or she is bored, it is a charge to which the parent immediately pleads guilty and accepts the penalty to provide years of constant stimulation until the child turns eighteen, or at the point when the child gets a diagnosis of attention-deficit disorder, whichever comes first. At that point, the parent will be required to medicate the child in order to increase their ability to focus on more and more stimulation.

Now, stop and think a moment about the word "stimulation." There are marketing efforts to encourage us to stimulate ourselves with food, and once we are overstimulated, we are sold all kinds of diets. There are marketing efforts to gamble or use alcohol. Once we are overstimulated, they tell us that we need to go to professionals to deal with these problems. If our minds become overstimulated, we can no longer focus. Somebody is waiting there to sell us drugs to take care of that problem.

Quite simply, there are people out there who make a lot of money in creating problems for people. People make more money in solving those problems. Unfortunately, there is very little money made in teaching people how to avoid that problem in the first place.

It all starts with practicing boredom. If you are in a car for six hours on a boring highway, you are supposed to be bored. If the kids spew out the CrankaTsuris "I am bored," then there is nothing to do but say, "I guess the boring drive works."

Boredom is crucial to our personal journey to creativity. When I watched the *Lawrence Welk Show*, it forced my mind to search for creative thoughts. If you are sitting in class and the teacher is doing her best to put you to sleep, you may learn, through your doodling, that you have the talent to be an amazing artist. If you are learning to play an instrument, it can be boring to play the same notes repeatedly for hours and hours of practice.

The reason for this boredom torture is that it can lead to a big reward of being able to play beautiful music. At some point, you are not only playing beautiful music, but you may be creating your own beautiful music. If you are trying to learn a new language, it may feel like weight training. It may hurt a bit, but those thinking muscles are getting stronger.

Think about that for a second. It is a bit counterintuitive. Your brain is telling you to stop doing the thing that is exactly what is good for the brain. Your brain will also tell you to do something that is bad like "have another drink" or "eat another bonbon." Always think of the brain as being two separate brains: one is the smart brain, and the other brain is much less so. Your job is to decide about the work that you have to do to give the smart brain a louder voice.

If there are continuous CrankaTsuris battles over boredom in your house, the strategy is to turn boredom into a practice or a house rule. Create a new normal. Have a quiet time, a reading time or some time of the day where you can simply daydream. Start a writing journal. Think of what would inspire you. We are making the brain muscles stronger, even if the not-so-smart brain says it wants something else.

Even more important, the practice of boredom is also the practice of patience. Patience leads to tolerance and kindness. It leads to being able to slow down thoughts in our mind when self-diagnosing the CrankaTsuris within ourselves and to be better prepared with empathy when we are on the receiving end of a loved one's CrankaTsuris. The more you practice boredom, the fewer CrankaTsuris episodes you will have because of boredom. The fewer CrankaTsuris you have over boredom, the less you will have of all kinds of CrankaTsuris.

This is the ultimate path to effective crankiness.

23

CUSTOMER CARE CRANKATSURIS

Customer Care CrankaTsuris—this is something we all experience when we have a problem and we call up a Customer Care Representative to solve the problem. We also do this despite having the knowledge that we have tried this many times before, and it never turns out well. As I mentioned before, "Insanity is doing the exact same thing over and over again and expecting a different result." Well, since we all continue to call up that very helpful customer care representative, this must mean that we truly are all insane.

I do want to walk through the Customer Care CrankaTsuris. However, before I do, I want to put something out there as a backdrop. You see, based on my career as an attorney, and I can tell you that there are many laws out there trying to protect people from robocalls.

As I am a consumer myself, I am all in favor of laws to protect consumers. However, I have to say, that this particular robocall law must have been concerned for those people who own a phone, but unfortunately missed the instructions part in the manual for how a person should actually hang up the phone. I guess there are some people out there who just never figured that part out. It turns out that our legislatures worked overtime together with bipartisan support to draft this particular law for this part of our population.

After reading this chapter, I ask all of you to call up your representative and tell them that you want the Customer Care CrankaTsuris Protection Act passed immediately. This is vital to our national interest. The gross domestic product would skyrocket because we would all become much happier and more efficient. We would be working instead of sitting for hours while being placed on hold and then walking away frustrated and depleted. Medical bills would drop significantly. We would all be nicer to each other because we would know there was someone on the other side of a telephone who can actually be helpful.

I am ready to sit before Congress and testify about my own experience of going through this maze of torment. Just the other day, I called up customer care because I had a question about a bill that I had in my hand in front of me.

Yes. The bill had the phone number right on the bill. However, they can never just give you just the phone number to call. They give you the phone number in block letters set in huge bold print. I do not know why they give us the letters in the first place. Even more frustrating than that, the number you actually need to dial is always in tiny barely readable print.

I am taking this example from an actual bill:

"For Customer Service: Call 1 (800) GET-HELP or 1 (800) 438-4357.

After spending fifteen minutes looking for my magnifying glass so that I can actually read the phone number, I called up my customer care representative. It started out pretty well. They wanted to know if I speak English or Spanish. I found out later that this question had no relationship to the language that the customer care representative spoke. This did not bother me at the time. I considered it a nice gesture. They then asked for the fourteen-digit account number and the seven-digit invoice number, my zip code, the last four digits of my social security number, and my secret six-digit numeric phone password. It took about ten minutes, but this did not bother me at the time. You do not want to play around with private financial stuff, I thought to myself.

The next thing I heard was this; "the phone call may be recorded for quality assurance." After many years of experience, I have reached the conclusion that the recording has nothing whatsoever to do with quality assurance. However, it did please me to hear about the recording of the phone call.

You see; if you have not yet noticed, I am Jewish, and when Jewish people pass away, they have a seven-day period of mourning called "sitting Shiva." So when I pass away, I expect that I will be able to collect all the recordings I have been on that were recorded for the purpose of quality assurance, and the length of those recordings should be about seven days, exactly the amount of time that people are required, under Jewish law, to mourn.

When people will sit Shiva after my passing, they will truly feel the grief, and pain, and there will be lots of sobbing—which is exactly what is required for this time of mourning. How will they be able to do this? They will be able to do this because I will have all those quality- assurance phone recordings playing throughout the week. They will all know of my suffering. When the recordings end, so can the period of mourning.

After I put in all my information, the recorded voice on the other side of the phone ask me another question: "Are you willing to take a three-minute survey after this phone call?" I always say no. It is not about the time—OK, it is a little bit about the time. However, I feel that if they have recorded the phone call for quality assurance, they can just listen to the entire phone call (which we all know they do), and they can fill out the survey themselves. "You have the recording. How do you think it all turned out?"

The recorded voice came on again and said, "Please listen to the menu closely because the options have changed." I was hoping to speak to a human, but I will listen to the menu. However, I have a question about this. I have been doing this customer care phone call stuff for years and years, and the options have all changed. They are always changing. I never hear about the options remaining the same as before. There must be a person at every company whose only job is to get on the phone and change the options every single day. Why do they even have to tell me that the options have changed in the first place? Just give me the menu. This never happens in a restaurant.

"Excuse me! Waiter! We have been waiting fifteen minutes for a menu. Can we get a menu?"

"Sorry, sir, we cannot give you a menu because our options have not changed!"

At this point, I never have a lot of patience to hear all of the options. I always press the number one, no matter what. The options usually are longer than the menu at the Cheesecake Factory. I am an inpatient person, by nature. I do not have all day.

Option number one is billing, so lucky me. I have a question about billing, so option one must be the correct choice. Unfortunately, after pressing option number one, I get a new menu of various recorded information about the bill, everything that is already in the bill that I was holding in my hand and had a question about. At the end of that menu, they tell me to press pound to go back to the previous menu. I press pound. Now, I have no choice but to listen to the entire twenty-minute rendition of the Cheesecake Factory menu, and it is only at the end that the recording says, "If you want to speak to a representative, stay on the line."

I stay on the line. However, half the time when I stay on the line, at this point, the call just disconnects. They hang up on me. That day I was lucky. They did not hang up. I can tell because they start blasting pleasant music in my ear. After two minutes, I hear someone talking. It is a recorded voice: "Do you know that you can get the same award-winning, high-quality customer care service by simply going online at www.confusinganduselesscustomercare.com?"

I say to myself, "Yes, and that is why I am calling. I went online.

It was both confusing and useless. However, I should have taken that to be a clue as to the service I was going to get."

There is more music and then a recorded voice comes on again: "Your call is very important to us. It will be taken in the order received."

This is very confusing to me. I ask myself; "How is my call very important to them?" I was just calling about a question on my bill. I hope they do not expect me to give them advice on how to double their profits. I realized another thing. If my call is very important, it only makes sense that I will be talking with a very important person.

I get a bit nervous now. Perhaps, the President of the Company will answer my call! No, wait! I think to myself that if my call is so very important, and I am going to be talking with the President, something here is very wrong. My call should not be taken in the order the call was received. They should tell me that that I will have my phone call placed first in line!

After waiting two hours, after finding out that I was eighty-third in line, the representative finally answers. It becomes immediately obvious that this person can barely speak English or understand the language. The representative asks me for my name. "Steven Joseph", I answer. "How do you spell that?" she asks. I spell out my name. She reads it back incorrectly. Then, after the fifth attempt, she finally gets the spelling of my name right. I cannot even begin to imagine what would have happened if I had some weird sounding thirty-nine consonants and difficult to spell name.

The representative again asks me for my fourteen-digit account number, my seven-digit invoice number, my zip code, the last four digits of my social security number, and my six-digit numeric phone password. I once again supply this information, and then the customer care representative replies, "Can I place you on a brief hold while I try to find your account?"

"Sure. Do I have a choice?" I say.

"Also, can I get a callback number in case we get disconnected?"

I give this person my callback number. I have to say that these are the only people who ask for a callback number, because for some unknown reason, these are the only people who hang up on me from time to time. However, do you know what? They never call back. They just ask me for the number to make me feel a bit more secure about the possibility of this person coming back on to talk to me.

Because of this, I make sure to get her call back number. She gives me the same number that I called: 1 800 Get Help. Uggh.

This time, amazingly enough, the customer care representative gets back on the phone. I ask the question. The answer is that he or she does not understand the question. I try again. After the fifth time rephrasing the question, the customer care representative tells me that they are unable to help me with my question. He or she then asks, "Have you tried going online to take care of this issue?"

"Yes!" I scream. It is a TyrantoCrankaTsuris scream because I no longer have any patience.

In a final feeble attempt to try to console me, the customer care representative asks, "Is there anything else I can help you with?"

I reply with another CrankaTsuris; "Anything else? That would imply that you helped me on the first thing! You helped me with nothing! I was four hours on the phone and I got nothing accomplished! Do you really want me to try again? Yes, wait! There is something you can help me with."

The customer care representative asks curiously, "What is it?"

"The quality assurance recording—I need it for my Shiva, the Jewish period of mourning. I can pay for expedited shipping because after this phone call there is going to be some mourning very soon. And also, if you can listen to the recording yourself after we get off the phone, you can complete the customer service survey—that would be great too!"

Let us pass the Customer Care CrankaTsuris Protection Act today!

CRANKATSURIS KRYPTONITE

CrankaTsuris kryptonite—we all know what that is: somebody, usually a family member, will say something or do something that triggers a very big CrankaTsuris. There is even anxiety before you face this because you know it is kryptonite and you happen to come from the planet Krypton. Unfortunately, it is not only that. When you arrived from Krypton, you did not come with all the superpowers.

Superman, oddly enough, was never curious about kryptonite. It did not make any difference to Superman that kryptonite almost killed him in the previous episode that was on a week before. Sure enough, a week later, after his close encounter with death, he would go straight back to crime fighting in the next episode. I always wished there were a Superman episode that had him go to the doctor to see if he could do anything about this allergic reaction.

"Doc, is there anything you can give me? I tried Flonase and Benadryl. They do not help a bit. OK, Tylenol does help a little with the X-ray vision, but otherwise, I am a complete mess. I feel weak and tired, and I cannot even move. You must help me, Doc. Can you maybe give me a steroid? This is killing me!"

Unlike Superman, we need to get curious about our own

kryptonite. What is it that triggers us? We all have those buttons, and our arch-villains, typically close family members, know exactly how to press them.

We know what these buttons are. There are the critical, judgmental parents or children. There are those people who do and say certain things that we, because we happen to be sane and normal, do not say and do. Sometimes, we can have a low tolerance for this, simply because we have a complete lack of comprehension as to why any normal person would say or do this thing.

On top of that, they will regard you as being the crazy person because you are the person with this complete lack of comprehension. Frustration builds, and out comes the CrankaTsuris after close exposure to this kryptonite. The response from this beloved family member or this arch-villain is to expose you to additional doses of CrankaTsuris kryptonite.

You return home from this wonderful experience. What is the feeling inside you? It feels like this experience has completely shredded your brain. Many strong people with unique superpowers of their own have had this experience. They have reached the conclusion that they simply will not expose themselves to this anymore. "We are never going to go to Aunt Ruthie's house again for Thanksgiving!"

Now, while avoidance can be a solution, think about Superman for a second. He never said, "I can't do this crime fighting thing anymore. It is just not worth it. Now, every petty criminal has kryptonite. When they graduate from Criminal Injustice School, they get a box of kryptonite with their diploma. Do you know that they even have synthetic kryptonite? How can that be legal? The Second Amendment, the right to bear arms, did not include the right to bear kryptonite! Moreover, there is nothing wrong with writing obituary columns for the *Daily Planet*! It's a perfectly respectable profession!"

Superman kept fighting, and on many occasions, he came very close to being kaput. Do you remember the first Superman movie when Lex Luther put the kryptonite necklace around Superman's neck and then, pushed him into his indoor pool? I thought he was a goner!

So, for Superman's sake, let us keep fighting. Explore the CrankaTsuris, and even talk about the kryptonite with your loved ones. Instead of the super-strength kryptonite, we expose each other to, maybe we can agree on using a milder version that will be less harmful.

There is one other thing you can do: keep it simple. Whenever you find that you may be in serious risk of kryptonite exposure, decide that you will respond one way and on way only. Think of this as being consistent and like wearing a protective lead jacket that will help you ward off the effects of kryptonite.

Also, check in and get as much sympathy as you can from all the loved ones who did not come from the planet Krypton and are asymptomatic. They may see things you do not see. They can help slow it down.

This is very important. Some of these people do not react well. They do not realize that you had some exposure to the CrankaTsuris kryptonite. They do not understand. They get critical. Again, you have to remind them of Jimmy Olsen and Lois Lane.

When the bad guys locked Superman in a lead covered room with a kryptonite chain around his neck, Jimmy and Lois always somehow managed to come to Superman's aid. They helped him out with the kryptonite problem. Imagine if Lois Lane had said, "You know what? I am so tired of your kryptonite issue! Screw this, Jimmy. Let's call Batman and Robin!"

Once you are consistent, slow it down and get lots of compassion from loved ones. CrankaTsuris kryptonite may not be curable. However, you need to remember this. You will always need to deal with and control those CrankaTsuris kryptonite issues. Know why this is so important: your family may be coming out with the synthetic and more powerful versions of the original kryptonite every single day! You need to be well prepared!

CHAPTER 25

TAG TEAM CRANKATSURIS

As a kid, I watched professional wrestling. It was a chance for my older brother to bond with me. We would watch the matches, and afterwards, my brother has to try out all of the wrestling moves on me. Of course, it never mattered that the announcer would always warn the TV viewers not to try these wrestling moves at home. That only provided my brother with even more encouragement. I quickly learned that the sleeper hold does not really put you to sleep, but I did discover that it made it very hard to breathe.

The best matches to watch were the ones that involved wrestlers who wrestled, as a tag team: the British Bulldogs and the Hart Foundation are two tag teams that come to mind. Each partner knew every move that the other made. They beautifully choreographed their matches. These wrestlers were real athletes and acrobats. It was more than just beating someone into a pulp in a steel cage, with a steel chair and a steel plate inside the arm sleeve.

It was actually, while watching these fabulous matches, that I discovered professional wrestling is fake. Every match was always the same. The bad guys, who were always way bigger than the good guys, would get one of the good guys into their corner and start beating the poor trapped wrestler until the wrestler became semiconscious.

The play-by-play announcer would start to criticize the referee for allowing this to go on. The bad guys were experts in distracting the referee. So of course, the referee never gets to see any illegal moves.

The beat-up wrestler, in a valiant effort, almost made it to his corner to tag his partner. Just when he was only inches away, the bad guys pulled back the beat-up wrestler into the other corner for another vicious beating. After five minutes went by, while you were wondering how this wrestler was even alive, he somehow got the intestinal fortitude to make it to his corner and tag his partner. Yay!

Oops! Once again distracted, this time by the bad guys' manager, the referee does not see the tag. The referee now finally takes control, and admonishes the tagged partner to go back to his corner. Meanwhile, once again, the bad guys pull back this poor beaten down partner into the opposing side's corner, where he gets his third beating in the course of twenty minutes.

After this two-on-one mugging, any normal humans would find themselves placed unconscious on a stretcher and the ambulance would take him straight to the hospital. Nevertheless, our hero somehow manages to get a sliver of energy to finally slip out of the clutches of death, make it to his corner, and finally make a legal tag of his partner.

On a scale of one to ten, the partner has it turned up to one hundred. He flies over the ropes and into the ring. He clotheslines one bad guy and then another. Next, he uses a flying drop kick and another. Little birdies start flying over the bad guys' heads, and the partner grabs the two bad guys by their hair and bashes their heads together, noggin to noggin. Everyone is going crazy and cheering for their hero.

The "fresh" new wrestler then makes the tag again. His partner has completely recovered from the three beatings. As anybody would have expected, the injury-recovered partner does not need an examination by the doctors to determine if he has a concussion or other brain injury. It is clear that this super human is now completely rejuvenated. He shows no signs of any injuries whatsoever. Of course, this is what we all can expect from a three-minute rest. He finishes the business, and pins one of the other wrestlers, who is now down, while his partner chases the other bad guy away. The match is over. The good guys win!

Why am I telling you this? Because this is actually what we wish would happen. So much CrankaTsuris finds us on the receiving end. That causes us to release our own CrankaTsuris. Here, it would be our fantasy to be able to tag our partner and have them make everything okay, even after getting double-teamed and triple-teamed with CrankaTsuris from the bad guys over and over again.

It is more likely that your partner was also stuck in the wrong corner and then, getting a bit of a beating. Both you and your partner find yourselves completely depleted. There is nothing left. There may still be a TyrantoCrankaTsuris out there with lots of energy to let out even more CrankaTsuris.

Think about this. Neither person is feeling safe, which leaves only one truth about this situation: when someone does not feel safe, that person are more likely to cause harm. Because of this fact, this is the important time to become tag team champions. Begin to choreograph the moves, anticipate the CrankaTsuris, and most importantly, name the CrankaTsuris. Name the CrankaTsuris you receive and the CrankaTsuris you want to give. Have your partner do the same.

Once you know all of the CrankaTsuris out there, each person will know when to make the tag. Practice this with compassion. No tag team ever became champions unless both partners had compassion for the other when they were in trouble. That is even when it is all fake. Life, of course, happens to be very real.

"So we learned to be careful not to express our inner TyrantoCrankaTsuris or TyrantoKvetchaTsuris too often—just the right amount to keep the planet happy and not too cranky."

CRANKATSURIS CATERPILLAR

If the TyrantoCrankaTsuris had a best friend, it would be the CrankaTsuris Caterpillar. I happen to think that the CrankaTsuris Caterpillar is almost the perfect metaphor for our own CrankaTsuris.

The CrankaTsuris Caterpillar spends its life crawling through the weeds and the trees. The CrankaTsuris Caterpillar moves slowly through the woods. He crawls in constant fear that, one day, he will be eaten by birds and ladybugs. The typical CrankaTsuris Caterpillar has sixteen legs, which means sixteen feet! I imagine the following conversation with my two CrankaTsuris Caterpillars, Zig and Zag.

> "Whoever thought it was a good idea to put sixteen feet on a caterpillar was nuts! You know that I missed school all week, just getting the dirt out from under my toes! My parents, who I love, can only afford two pairs of shoes for each of us. I put one pair on the front two and the other pair on the back two. The rest of the feet—ugh—by the end of the week, they are disgusting. And my family has one bucket for ten kids, so I only get one day a week to soak my feet,

and as you know, it is not easy to soak sixteen feet in one bucket," says Zig.

Zag says, "Have you tried slippers?"

"Slippers?"

"Yeah. I go to Target, and they have a 'buy one, get one free' deal on slippers. They are much cheaper than shoes. I put the slippers on all the middle feet, and that way, I can just walk with the front feet and slide with most of the others, and the back feet give me support."

Zig says, "Oh, I saw you with the slippers, trying to climb up the tree the other day. You were ahead of me. You know what happened. The slippers that kept falling off and hitting me on the head! I was wondering what that was!"

"Oops, sorry," Zag says.

"No, no, I think it's good. I heard about the slippers, and birds do not like to eat caterpillars wearing slippers. Thanks."

Enough with the feet—the feet are the least of CrankaTsuris Caterpillars' worries. As they get close to becoming a butterfly, all of their insides turn to liquid, forming a pupa. They do not know why. They just know that they do not feel well. "Maybe I had some bad grass," Zig says. "Zag, do you hear me? Are you there?"

Zag ends up getting trapped in his little cocoon. "I am in here! It is so dark! Where am I? I must have had the bad grass too, became I am turning into liquid mush. Now look at me!"

Before Zig can answer, he too turns into a cocoon, and they both slip into unconsciousness.

Now, I said that the CrankaTsuris Caterpillar was almost the perfect metaphor for our own CrankaTsuris. The reason I said that this was an "almost perfect" metaphor is because a caterpillar has no clue that he or she will turn into a beautiful butterfly. Of course, we always love to tell Little Johnny and Little Susie that they are little caterpillars that will grow into beautiful butterflies!

So let us give the CrankaTsuris Caterpillar the knowledge that one day he may turn into a beautiful butterfly, can throw away the shoes and the slippers, and just fly away. That is, if the CrankaTsuris Caterpillar is not eaten or become frozen in the winter.

In the meantime, the poor CrankaTsuris Caterpillar sits at home and watches all those TV shows about beautiful butterflies. He did have a favorite caterpillar show. Guess what happened to the only caterpillar show. Of course, the show was cancelled. The worst, however, was when some of his friends became butterflies.

His parents said to him, "I hear your friend Big Marty got a good summer job at Butterfly World. Why are you not able to get a job there? A teenage caterpillar should be working in the summer!"

"Oh, and I hear that Little Stewie got into the Butterfly Academy. You did not even apply. There was a deadline. You look, but you only look after the deadline. Oy, our son the caterpillar."

It does not stop.

"Oh, what is that mark on your face? Have you been bitten by a ladybug again? Now, if you were a beautiful butterfly with wings, you would not have such problems!"

What makes this story funny and relatable is that the parents of the CrankaTsuris Caterpillar are themselves caterpillars. They never were and cannot become butterflies. It is precisely because they never became butterflies that they desperately want CrankaTsuris Caterpillar to be the first in the family to become a butterfly.

So much of our own CrankaTsuris comes from our caterpillar

mind. We all become stuck in the weeds, look at others flying around with their beautiful wings, and our caterpillar mind causes this form of CrankaTsuris suffering. That is why, when I go to the Village Zendo in New York City to meditate, our wonderful teacher, Roshi Enkio O'Hara, would refer to our bodies as a skin bag. You do not go to sit on a cushion and stare at a wall to work on your body. We work to develop our butterfly mind.

This reminds me of the butterfly mind when a friend of mine, Nupur Biswal, who recently, had me read her wonderful book, *Let's Celebrate 5 Days of Diwali* that describes the Indian holiday called the "Festival of Lights." Each day comes with a different kind of celebration, with different colors, tastes, and smells.

Before reading this simple but beautiful little book, I had never even heard of this holiday. However, I finished the book and felt absolute joy. It is a holiday when young and old get together. I realized that this is a holiday meant for only one reason: to help all of us cultivate our butterfly mind.

If we all try to spend a little time each day working on our butterfly mind, some magic happens. Our CrankaTsuris cocoon slowly disappears, and that is when we get to start growing our butterfly wings.

THE FLY IN THE OINTMENT
CRANKATSURIS

Once upon a time, there lived a man named Shmulie Shmendrick. Shmulie Shmendrick was a special man because he owned the one ointment factory in the entire town. Shmulie Shmendrick had an ointment for everything. If you had a rash, he had an ointment for that. If you had sore muscles, he had an ointment for that. If you had a chest cold, it was not a problem. He had an ointment for that as well.

Because he had an ointment for every possible condition, Shmulie Shmendrick was the most beloved man in town. There was not a single person in town that did not use at least three of Shmulie Shmendrick's ointments. The ointments were sold in jars, and it was very typical to find a fly in each of these jars of ointments. People never complained about the fly in the ointment. This is because they were all convinced that it was the fly in the ointment that gave the ointment its magical powers.

One day, Shmulie Shmendrick went to the finest restaurant in the town for dinner. He was seated at his special table, and he immediately ordered a cup of the fly soup. After the waiter brought over the soup, Shmulie Shmendrick looked at the cup of soup, and saw a fly staring at him, flapping its wings.

The fly said to Shmulie Shmendrick; "I was flying all day looking for my family. I got tired from flying and looking all over. Finally, I asked this ladybug if she would know where they are. You know what she told me. She told me that they all ended up in one of your jars of ointment. Is that true?"

Shmulie Shmendrick was frightened by the talking fly, and immediately summoned the waiter.

"Yes, Mr. Shmendrick. How can I help you?" asked the waiter

"There is a fly in my soup." Mr. Shmendrick exclaimed.

"But, Mr. Shmendrick. You ordered the fly soup." explained the waiter.

Mr. Shmendrick instructed the waiter: "Just bring over a cup of the fly soup, but without the flies."

In order to make his customer happy, the waiter came over and Shmulie Shmendrick was then presented with a big bowl of fly-free fly soup. However, he was so frightened by the talking fly that he was determined to sell jars of ointment without any flies. In fact, he personally inspected every jar of ointment, and if the jar of ointment had a fly, he would throw the jar of ointment out.

Unfortunately, Shmulie Shmendrick soon found out that selling jarred ointment without any flies was quite expensive, and he was unable to make a profit on selling these fly-free jars of ointment. Eventually, Shmulie Shmendrick had no choice, but to sell his beloved company.

Shelly Sheygitz saw the ad in the paper notifying everyone that the ointment company was up for sale. Immediately, Shelly Sheygitz ran to the ointment factory, and expressed his interest to Shmulie Shmendrick in buying his company. In fact, he was so interested, he told Shmulie Shmendrick to name his price.

Shmulie Shmendrick replied to Shelly Sheygitz: "Mr. Sheygitz. I am not interested in the price. I am interested in one thing only. You have to promise me that if you buy this company, you have to sell ointment without any flies in the ointment."

Mr. Sheygitz was very excited with this offer, and he offered his hand to Mr. Shmendrick.

"Deal!" he said.

Soon after, Shelly Sheygitz took over the ointment factory, and immediately went from selling the ointment in the large jars that Shmulie Shmendrick had used to tubes of ointment. Apparently, the flies were not able to fit inside the tubes. More importantly, the tubes were much cheaper than the large jars used by Shmulie Shmendrick. Shelly Sheygitz lowered the price of all the ointments by half, making everyone in town excited.

Everybody in town loved the tubes, and forgot about how they once thought that the fly in the ointment contained magical powers. They now believed that if there was a fly in the ointment, it must be impure and should be thrown away immediately.

Poor Shmulie Shmendrick was now remembered in town as the man who sold the dirty ointment. Everyone in town scorned him. A child was walking with his mother, and when the mother saw that Shmulie Shmendrick was approaching them, they immediately crossed to the other side of the street.

"Who is that man"? the child asked.

The mother replied, "That is the man who put the fly in the ointment!"

"Ooh, that is gross!" the child responded.

Shmulie Shmendrick died penniless and with a broken heart. Shelly Sheygitz, who made a fortune with the ointment factory, came to Shmulie Shmendrick's bedside just before he passed.

Shmulie Shmendrick's last words were "If I only knew about the tubes."

To this day, people have big problems with the person who put the fly in the ointment. This is interesting because you never really hear complaints about flies at a picnic. We do not want mosquitoes or bees showing up because they bite. Those ants can be really annoying at a picnic. If we have a picnic, and the only flying object we encountered was a fly, we would all consider the picnic a huge success.

With our own CrankaTsuris, we become too accustomed with not wanting to feel any discomfort. We train ourselves instinctively wanting to swat the fly. Some bugs do bite. These bugs can cause severe pain, and perhaps, there should be some consideration given to swatting them. However, we are not dealing with this particular form of severe CrankaTsuris. Any such discussion would open up a hornet's nest.

Yet, even with the biting bugs, we always should remind ourselves that we need the bees to bring us the honey. Our survival depends on the bees, and the sweetness they provide.

Because of this, instead of looking at the fly in the ointment as some impurity, we should begin to look at ourselves and remind each other that we are all flies in the ointment at some point. We each get lost in the CrankaTsuris ointment, and sometimes, we feel stuck. However, once we think of ourselves as being the fly in the ointment, we can learn to help each other get out of the ointment.

And, what happens sometimes when we get stuck in the ointment? We learn that even the ointment can have magical powers and help us be more effective in dealing with our personal CrankaTsuris.

28

CAN OF WORMS CRANKATSURIS

This is a story I like to share with you that can really be helpful with the effective management of your CrankaTsuris.

I was set to meet with the big boss. I never met the big boss before so I was rather nervous. People in the organization were also nervous about me meeting with the big boss. Because they were even more nervous than I was, the organization set up a meeting between Big Tony and myself. Big Tony sat me down, and the discussion went like this:

> Big Tony: Now, when you meet the Big Boss, the one thing that you have to make sure not to do is to bring up the "thing." You bring up the thing, and the Big Boss gets very upset about the thing.

> Me: Big Tony. You can count on me. I will not mention a single word about the thing. I do not even know what the thing is. I never heard of the thing, and if I heard about the thing, I forgot already what the thing was. There will be no mention of the thing. I do have one question.

Big Tony: What is the question?

Me: I am just curious. What exactly happens if I mention the thing?

Big Tony: It is terrible. What I can tell you is that if you mention the thing, it will open up the can.

Me: Well. What is in the can?

Big Tony: I should not tell you what is in the can. What is in the can is even worse than the thing.

Me: Is it a can of sunshine?

Big Tony: Sunshine? What are you talking about?

Me: I went to Florida once, and I was at the souvenir shop. They were selling cans of Florida sunshine. I bought a whole case, and when I got home, I opened up a can. There was no sunshine in it. It was completely empty. I spent almost three hundred dollars on the case of empty cans. My friends still rag on me for that. It has become a thing.

Big Tony: It is worse than that. I will tell you. Worms. It would open up a can of worms.

Me: Worms! Oh no. That is worse! I will definitely not mention the thing."

I have to admit. I do not understand what the big deal is about opening up a can of worms. First, if people do not like to open a can of worms, then answer this question. Why did they put the worms in the can in the first place? Second, if a can of worms opened up, what is the worst thing that could happen? One worm crawls out, and you put the worm back in to the can. It is not very complicated.

I could understand why someone would not want to open up a can of bees. If you opened up a can of bees, all the bees would fly out. A few of the bees would end up stinging you. You definitely do not want to open up a can of bees.

Even though you would never want to open up a can of bees, to add insult to your bee-bitten injury, they actually named a can of tuna fish after the bumblebee. While the worm helped catch the tuna, the bumblebee gets to be on the can. I hear that the bumblebee is even on a can of salmon. This is simply unfair.

To correct this injustice and inequity, I have decided to start my own tuna fish company "Wormy Tuna." It will be a big hit. I will sell cans of tuna, with all of the worms that the caught tunas were unable to digest. I even have the sales pitch. "If they can stick a worm in a bottle of tequila, a worm in a can of tuna will not kill you."

As I promised in the beginning, there is a message with this story that will help you in the effective management of your CrankaTsuris. You will discover that on many occasions, the CrankaTsuris feels like you are holding a can of stingy bees inside your head. All you want to do is to open up the can, and let all the bees out. The more they bite everyone around you, the better.

Of course, it may not be very helpful to have everyone around stung in such a fashion. Here is what you should do instead. Grab a can and sit with the can for a few minutes. Imagine that the inside of the can is filled with those nasty bees. Rub the top of the can for a few minutes, and now, begin to imagine that worms replace the bees.

Opening up a can of worms is not that bad after all.

FATHER'S DAY CRANKATSURIS

Happy Father's Day! Father's Day always brings to mind the Father's Day I had with my father two years ago, when I was visiting him in his assisted-living home in Delray Beach, Florida.

Like many people in their nineties, my father had to accept wearing dentures because his teeth were either not working for him or no longer residing inside his mouth. I can tell you that there is nothing more adorable than old people are with no teeth.

I remember visiting both my parents, when my mom was alive, and we were about to say goodnight and head back to the hotel. They were both sitting on the couch in their pajamas, and their dentures were sitting in the cups in the bathroom. Anybody who has old relatives with dentures knows what I am talking about. Whether they are smiling or not, their faces look like one giant smile. There is a gleefulness in the expressions when the words come out of their mouth. Sentences like "I have really bad diarrhea!" are words taken over by a delicious sweetness.

Now, as adorable as that scene was, there can be nothing worse than when my father would decide to take his teeth out when we were at a restaurant. Whenever I visit, lunch is always at Flakowitz, a Jewish-style deli in Boynton Beach, and my father always has the same order: a corned beef sandwich and a Sprite.

I could ask you to picture this. Instead, I recommend trying hard not to picture this; it is not a very pretty picture when your father takes his teeth out halfway through a corned beef sandwich, and you find yourself staring at teeth on a table with mustard, chewed up corn beef, and the seeds from the rye bread. (We said no seeds!) This would happen on a regular basis when visiting my father, and I somehow got used to the display.

Getting back to Father's Day 2017—I took my father out for Italian food at a nearby Italian restaurant. The teeth came out midway. My father placed his teeth in a napkin, and I thought I saw my father put the napkin in his pocket when we left the restaurant.

When we got back to the assisted-living home, I asked my father, "Do you have your teeth?" My father reached into his pocket and took out the napkin—no teeth. He desperately checked his other pockets—no teeth. I ran back to the car and drove straight to the restaurant while my father waited anxiously, sitting outside the assisted-living home.

I got back to the restaurant and explained to the host that I thought my father had left his teeth at the table where we were sitting. The host said, "Your father is the third person this week that lost his teeth here."

I was happy about this news and said anxiously, "I just hope you can find my father's teeth."

She came back, shaking her head. "Sorry, no teeth."

I drove back to the residence. By now, all the aids working there knew about my father's teeth dilemma. When I said that the restaurant did not have the teeth, a beautiful Haitian aide came out with black latex gloves. She handed the gloves to me and said, "You go straight back there and look for your father's teeth. Here are gloves. Check all their garbage."

"Yes, ma'am!"

Armed with the pair of black latex gloves, I headed straight back. I explained to the host that the aide sent me back with strict orders to check all of the restaurant's garbage. I was not taking no for an answer.

The host took me out back, past the kitchen to the dumpster. Surrounded by flies, mosquitoes, and bees, I waded through the half-eaten pizza, mussel shells, chewed-up pasta, cheese, and leftover veal parmesan. Because I had to wade my arms through the sauces, the sauces made each arm looked as if they had been covered in blood.

After fifteen minutes of wading through the mess, I felt as if something was biting me. "Please be the teeth and not a rat burrowed into this mess!" I said. Pulling my arm slowly up, just like an angler, winding the string out of the water to see his catch, my father's teeth emerged.

I ran through the kitchen, screaming, "I have the teeth! I have the teeth!" All the cooks and workers stopped what they were doing and applauded. I was a hero. I was bringing back the teeth! This was my rock-star moment!

Driving home, a thought occurred to me: *What if these teeth were not my father's teeth but someone else's. Eh, he will not notice.* I continued driving back.

"I got the teeth! I got the teeth!" Outside the assisted-living home, they were all dancing in the street. My father was beaming with such joy. To this day, I could not remember him ever having been that happy. He got up slowly and gave me a big hug. Taking the teeth, he was about to put them back in his mouth.

"No, Dad! We have to wash them first!"

It is funny how some CrankaTsuris can turn out to be some of the best memories. Happy Father's Day!

30

LOST LUGGAGE CRANKATSURIS

In *The Last Surviving Dinosaur: The TyrantoCrankaTsuris*, all the relatives compete for the gold medal at the Tsuris Olympics. "If I had your tsuris, I would be doing cartwheels! Nobody can outdo my tsuris!" However, when we hear about others' tsuris, and primarily when they crank out their tsuris for us to listen to until we become tsuris tartare, we do not necessarily start to think, *it could have been worse!* We tend to diminish the tsuris or problems of others.

Again, I brought back to the days when I was living in Pittsburgh after law school. I have to remind you once again of all my tsuris. My girlfriend dumped me just before Christmas. Someone stole my brand new car on New Year's Eve. When I returned to work the following Monday, I was fired from my job. Then, just when I thought things could not get any worse, I allowed my roommate to treat me to a Three Stooges Midnight Movie Marathon. I have to say this again. Three hours of Moe, Larry, and Curly does not mend the broken heart of a twenty-seven-year-old!

My roommate, seeing that the movie marathon sent me further into my abyss, said to me, "It could be worse. You could be diagnosed with a brain tumor and get hit by a truck!"

"How is that worse? If I get hit by a truck, it would put me out of my misery and take care of that brain tumor," I said.

More recently, last summer to be exact, I was flying with my girlfriend from Amsterdam to Tel Aviv on Tarom Air. Tarom Air is a Romanian airline, so it stops in Bucharest, its capital. My father is from Bucharest, so I was excited to at least to stop at the airport of my fatherland. I had used frequent flyer miles. Of course, by using frequent flyer miles, my options were limited, and Tarom Air was the only miles option available. That was really the only reason I was flying on Tarom Air.

We had checked four bags, and when we arrived at the baggage carousel at Ben Gurion Airport, only one of the four bags had arrived. It could have been worse—at least we got one bag.

They told us at the lost luggage window that it could take a week to ten days to recover our luggage. We were in Israel for only a week, so that forecast was not a good one. This would be a disaster. We were convinced that we would never see our luggage again. I pictured traveling back to Bucharest years later, and while walking through the streets, I would see all of our clothes being put on display at some local bazaar in Bucharest.

This is what I heard from my partner after we waited ninety minutes to find out that three large duffel bags would not be joining us: "Why couldn't we take a direct flight? We had to stop in Bucharest. We did not see Bucharest, except for that smoky airport. This is what you get when you pick the free flight! I will never trust you planning anything for as long as I live!"

Oy. I deserved that. Luckily, I was able to call up Delta, which is the airline we had booked the Tarom Air flight. They were able to tell me that they tracked the luggage, and they scheduled to have the luggage placed on the eight in the morning flight to Tel Aviv the next day, arriving at eleven in the morning. Well, I was going to be back at Ben Gurion at eleven o'clock.

I got to the airport and went to a special window for lost luggage.

I got to the front, and there was a young man at a desk with a phone. There were instructions in English to dial a number on the phone to ask about your bags. I got to the window after waiting a half an hour in line, and I dialed the number. There was no answer.

The young man told me to come back half an hour later and try again. I went to the back of the line, since it happened to be a half-hour line, and I eventually got to the front again—and the same thing happened.

This time, however, I knew that it was happening to everyone. Now, this time I was ready. There was no answer on the phone, and I said, "I am not going anywhere." Amazingly enough, the man went to the back of the room and, like the Wizard of Oz, the man behind the curtain, who I had been calling, appeared. He started to tell me that it was hopeless, and they would not be able to locate my luggage. I was ready.

"Not true! It just arrived on Tarom Air Flight 1160, carousel ten. Go, and check."

The man went back to look, and for the first time, I noticed all the other desperate people. There was a rabbi. He was wearing a long black coat and black hat. He was screaming at the top of his lungs, "I need my luggage for Shabbas! It has my Shabbas clothes! You have to help me!"

Behind him, a sweet old grandmother was standing on line. She was yelling, "I have my diabetes medication in my bag. I need my medication! I will die without my medication. You have to help me!"

Yet, the worst was a young woman behind the two others. She was flying to Israel to get married in Jerusalem, and apparently, her wedding dress was in her lost suitcase. She would not stop screaming. Her wedding was on Sunday. She announced to everyone who can hear that her wedding day was now completely ruined. Finally, the police had to come and carry her away.

After this spectacle, the man that went to carousel ten came back and told me, "You were right. Let me take you there." The three bags were there, and I gave each one of them a big hug, as if they were my lost children. The bags and I were reunited. While I was in the middle of my wildly grateful hug-fest, the man said to me, "You know you are very lucky. It could have been much worse!

31

HANSEL AND GRETEL CRANKATSURIS

At the end of *The Last Surviving Dinosaur: The TyrantoCrankaTsuris*, the father tells the daughter, "So we learned to be careful not to express our inner TyrantoCrankaTsuris or TyrantoKvetchaTsuris too often—just the right amount to keep the planet happy and not too cranky."

So now, I bring up Hansel and Gretel. With these two kids, there was tsuris to be sure, but they presented no symptom of any kind of CrankaTsuris or KvetchaTsuris.

To recount the story, apparently Hansel and Gretel's parents were not doing quite so well financially. At the time, everyone was going through hard times. Because everyone else was starving as well, they had reasoned that, rather than go to relatives or friends for help, it would be best to take Hansel and Gretel out into the forest to face a horrible and painful death. Death would also come slowly. The plan was that if they left Hansel and Gretel in the forest alone, eventually, they would be mauled and then eaten by wild animals.

They tried this twice. The first time Hansel was smart and overheard his parents. Rather than complain what terrible parents they had, or call Family Services or the police to report child abuse,

Hansel stuffed his pockets with pebbles, so when they were all the way out in the forest, Hansel and Gretel were able to find their way back home.

This failed attempt did not deter the parents from again trying to dump their kids in the forest. They probably even took a different route. However, because when Hansel dropped breadcrumbs instead of pebbles along the way, this time to get back home, a flock of birds ate the breadcrumbs and there were no pebbles to follow. Hansel and Gretel were now stuck in the forest.

Hansel and Gretel then found a wicked witch's house. The wicked witch expected Hansel and Gretel. Once Hansel and Gretel arrived, the wicked witch used wicked witch tricks, and she captures Hansel and Gretel. As it would happen, whenever a wicked witch captures young children, she throws them into the oven. Soon, of course, we find Hansel cooking away in the oven. The oven is set to three hundred and twenty five degrees Fahrenheit. This is the perfect temperature to cook Hansel Pie.

Luckily, the oven did not yet reach three hundred and twenty five degrees. That was because the wicked witch just started to preheat the oven and the oven was not too hot yet. Just before the oven reached a temperature of three hundred and twenty five degrees, Hansel tricks the witch, and the poor wicked witch ends up pushed into the oven by Hansel.

Hansel and Gretel then discovered the fabulous wealth the witch possessed: gold, jewels, and coins (not to mention the valuable property she owned, since it was a one of kind house).

The wicked witch did not have a will, and there was no executor of her estate, so Hansel and Gretel took the gold, jewels, and coins back to their parents. Hansel and Gretel did not seem bothered in the slightest by the fact that, on two separate occasions, their parents had attempted to cause their kids to face a premature and grisly death at the mouths and claws of wild beasts.

They lived happily ever after—uh-huh, right.

Just imagine this family scene if the parents had been successful. Let us go with it. Wild animals, in fact, ate both Hansel and Gretel. However, shortly thereafter, the grandparents show up unexpectedly.

Grandma says, "Surprise! We thought we would drop in to say hello. We missed our two delicious grandkids, Hansel and Gretel, and we brought some outfits for them and some toys."

Grandpa says, "Let me tell you, we skipped a couple of meals so we would be able to afford the presents. But, you know how much we love them! I can eat both of them up! They are so delicious! Where are they? Grandma and I want to give both of them great big hugs!"

Mother says to Father, "Do you want to tell them, or should I?"

"Uh-oh, could you tell them?" says Father.

Mother says, "I think you should tell them. It was your idea. And they are your parents!"

Father says, "My idea! We both agreed, and you said you were tired of cooking for them. OK, I will tell them."

Grandpa and Grandma both say, "Tell us what?"

"Well, it is like this. You know how things have been tough since I lost my job at the factory. Then, our meals were getting smaller and smaller, and you know how kids are. Their appetites were getting bigger and bigger. They were literally eating us out of house and home!" Father says.

"So where are they?" Grandma asks.

"We had the idea that it would be better for Hansel and Gretel to get eaten by wild animals, rather than to starve at home a slow death. We were afraid they would not stop eating, and we would also be dying a slow death from starvation," says Mother.

Grandpa says, "So they were eaten by wild animals?"

Father says, "Yes. Yes, that is right. Flesh, bones, everything, but not the clothing—the wild animals did not eat that."

Grandma says, "Wait a second. You said you were starving. We walked in here, and I smell delicious roasted meat, something I have never smelled before."

Mother says, "Yes, that is the good news. After we dropped Hansel and Gretel in the forest, and after they were eaten by wild animals, we were still hungry, so we decided, or I decided, to send your son out hunting."

Father says, "And I captured and killed the wild animals that ate Hansel and Gretel. Therefore, you can say, in a sense, Hansel and Gretel are here. It is just that they are here in spirit, as part of our dinner."

Grandpa and Grandma say, "Well, they smell delicious, and we are hungry. So, let's eat!"

> Of course, they ate happily ever after! (Alternatively, instead of saying they got to have their cake and eat it too, they got to have their kids and eat them too!)

Even if we assume Hansel and Gretel escaped the wicked witch and brought home to their parents this unexpected wealth, how do we really know that they lived happily ever after? Maybe the parents got greedy and took Hansel and Gretel out to the forest, close to the wicked witch's sister, who also happened to be wealthy; they thought that Hansel would trick the sister as well. However, the sister knew what had happened before, and she ordered a top-of-the-line oven that locked automatically and fit both Hansel and Gretel. The wicked witch's sister enjoyed stuffed Hansel and Gretel for Thanksgiving!

We read this story to our children many times over again. The illustrations are always wonderful, no matter what version. Yet, we never question the premise of the story. Parents behaved badly. Children never complained. Parents end up mightily rewarded in the end. Kids are happy. The parents have nothing for which that they need to ask for forgiveness. I guess that is why parents love the story: Parents acting badly. Children never complaining, no matter what! That is awesome!

Well, please do not get carried away with that. Try to read this story anew, with our CrankaTsuris and KvetchaTsuris in mind. This should prompt questions and challenges, as well as our desire to seek true justice and true peace. This should always be our way of thinking.

32

THE STRAW THAT BROKE THE CAMEL'S BACK CRANKATSURIS

If you plan to have an effective CrankaTsuris practice, it is important to know your history. It is true what they say. Those who do not learn history tend to repeat it.

When it comes to thinking about your CrankaTsuris practice, one history lesson to learn is the story about "The Straw that Broke the Camel's Back." Of course, we all know that there have been many camels who have had someone put a straw on their back. Unfortunately, many of these poor camels suffered the same fate. It broke their backs, and they never fully recovered.

The very first camel that had his back broken by a straw goes all the way back to Biblical times. This part of the story of Cain and Abel is the part that you did not learn in Sunday school.

They lived in the middle of the desert where there lived many camels. Cain was the hunter. Abel was the farmer. They fought about many things, but there was one thing that they both shared: their love for their beloved camel, who happened to have been named, Camel.

Cain came home one day from a long and successful hunting

trip. However, when he came home, he saw Abel on the ground, crying next to Camel, who was lying flat on the ground. His back was broken.

"What happened to Camel?" Cain asked Abel.

Abel replied; "Camel's back is broken!"

Annoyed, Cain said; "I can see that, but how?"

Abel explained; "Well, as you know, we are in the desert, and it is really hot. It feels like an oven. I so miss that Garden of Eden.

Anyway, you know that Bedouin neighbor we have, Abraham. He invited me into his tent, and he offered me a Pepsi."

Forgetting Camel for a second, Cain smiled. "That Abraham is such a nice man, and his wife is ninety years old. Are they still trying to have a baby?"

Abel laughed, and said; "It is very silly and cute, but I do not say anything. I play along, and give encouragement. I said I have a strong feeling that this could be the year. I even said to him, 'You say she is ninety years old. She does not look a day over eighty.'"

Cain then remembered about poor Camel. "So, tell me what happened to Camel. You said something about a Pepsi."

Abel replied; "Yes. Abraham offers me a Pepsi, but he had to excuse himself because it was that time again for Abraham to try to get his wife pregnant. So, he gives me a straw and it was a paper straw, mind you. Not plastic. I go out of the tent, and I put the straw down on Camel so that I could open the can of Pepsi, and the next thing I knew, I saw that the straw broke Camel's back."

Cain was angry. "How can you put a straw on Camel's back?" Cain cried.

Abel got defensive. "How am I supposed to know that a paper straw will break Camel's back? Besides, I see you all the time riding Camel around while you put your big butt on Camel!"

Cain shot back; "Who has a big butt? Do you know what? You have a straw butt. Camel hates your scrawny straw butt. Camel probably felt the straw, and thought it was your straw butt, and the straw freaked Camel out."

Abel tried to change the subject. "Can't we just give Camel some aspirin, or maybe Tylenol? How about we just put a Band-Aid on it?"

Cain shook his head. "No, you can't put a Band-Aid on a broken back. Camel would need a back operation. Back operations are not cheap, and they do not always work. Remember when Horse broke his back. He had to have five back surgeries. When the surgeons were done with Horse, do you know what he ended up looking like? He ended up looking like Camel."

Abel looked up with hope and a twinkle in his eyes. "So, I got an idea. We take Camel to get the back operation, and after the operation, he will look just like Horse used to look. We just start calling Camel "Horse", and Horse, we would call him 'Camel.'"

Cain looked at Abel, and said: "Yeah. That is an idea only if I can call you Dummy."

This is one of the most important reasons for why we all need to develop our CrankaTsuris practice. We all end up in life carrying other people's straw. When the official administers the wedding vows to the bride and groom, the Bride is never asked this question:

"Do you take this man with no straw, a little bit of straw, a moderate amount, or are you someone who can take a ton of straw from this man?"

Of course, given the choice, the Bride would always answer:

"Enough with the straw. I cannot handle any straw. He gave me enough straw while we were dating to last fifty years! But, do you know what? If I am required to take a straw with this deal, I want the straw with the spoon. You know. The straw they give you with a Slurpee. Slurpees are delicious. Especially in the summer!"

So, let us face it. Straw is a part of life. Before you started your CrankaTsuris practice, you were not able to carry much straw. Did you. Not only did you have a very weak back that could break in a second, but also, someone could take a lousy paper straw, put in on your back, and your back would then break into many pieces.

Now, imagine that you have a strong CrankaTsuris practice. What would it look like? I can tell you. You begin to see all or at least many of the different kinds of straw out there. You have straw conversations. You learn about other loved one's straws. You can even have a few bales of hay go on your back. You then begin to feel how much stronger your back has become, and if you bring your family along for the ride, they will too!

So, when your daughter asks for a piggyback ride, tell her to hop right on. However, remember this. Even with your CrankaTsuris practice working, just to be on the safe side, make sure she is not carrying a straw with her.

33

CRANKATSURIS MARATHON

On November 3, 2019, I ran the New York City Marathon. I was going into the marathon with twelve consecutive, sub-four-hour marathons under my belt, but unfortunately age (fifty-eight years!) and other factors caught up with me. I finished the marathon in four hours, twenty-two minutes, and twelve seconds.

However, there is a story to tell.

The signs were there the night before. People always talk about doing a great big pasta dinner the night before to carbo load, but I always go to the same Chinese restaurant and order their Gung-Ho special. Unfortunately, they were out of Gung-Ho. I was not worried. I always enjoyed their Mo-Jo ice cream for dessert. I would get two orders of Mo-Jo. Unfortunately, they were out of Mo-Jo too.

In the morning, I traveled to Staten Island, Gung-less, Ho-less, Mo-less, and Jo-less. I still was not worried. I was staring at the Verrazano Bridge, with all of its cylinders. I was determined to click on all of the cylinders on the bridge.

The starting gun sounded. Fifty-two thousand runners started their way across the bridge. All of them started clicking on all of the cylinders. It was very loud. You could barely hear yourself click. I was able to click on a few of the cylinders, but the loud noise of the clicking forced me to click my way to Brooklyn as fast as I could. I did try to use all of my fingers and all of my toes to click on as many cylinders as I could while on the bridge. However, the second I crossed the bridge, I noticed that the clicking caused my fingers and toes to blister—four more boroughs, and no more clicking on any cylinders. I had become click-less.

In addition, I was:

Gung-less,

Ho-less,

Mo-less,

and,

Jo-less.

Well, here is the serious and sad part of my story. On October 28, a week before, my former partner of twenty years, Elena, and mother of my daughter, Vita, received a diagnosis of ALS (amyotrophic lateral sclerosis), a terrible disease that just shuts down the body and for which there is no known cure. My heart was broken hearing the news. Elena had grown up with juvenile rheumatoid arthritis and dedicated her whole life, with all the Gung, Ho, and much Mo and Jo, to take on her arthritis through movement in dance, yoga, Alexander technique, and Feldenchrist movement. She was always an inspiration to me.

With this heavy heart, I pushed on through the five boroughs. I had the wonderful surprise of seeing my daughter, Vita, at mile nine, by the Brooklyn Academy of Music, and gave her a big hug. I cried like a baby running the next mile.

Feeling in me Elena's spirit of always fighting and pushing past and shattering any boundaries in front of her, I found that I did not need any Gung, Ho, Mo, or Jo. I had the thought of this special person, and knowing what a fight she had ahead, I was going to keep fighting too. I was going to cross the finish line with the hope that Elena gets to cross hers as well.

I pray every day that next year Elena will be able to click on all the cylinders. In 2021, I hope to be running both the Chicago and New York City marathons for Team Challenge ALS.

This is what I write in every TyrantoCrankaTsuris book, and it is never can be so truer than now: "Never be afraid to take on all those bigger and badder dinosaurs! With love, Steve."

34

THANKSGIVING CRANKATSURIS

I spend much of my day answering the same type of question, both in person and on the phone: "How is it going?" or "How are you doing?" or "What's going on?" or "How was your weekend?"

The answers are typically the "non-answer": "Hanging in there!" or "Almost Friday!" or "My weekend was too short!"

I notice that when I give the typical "sitting in neutral" response to the question and then I ask the same question in return, I get the exact same response: "Hanging in there too." Then we part ways. "Well, you have a great day!" to which the response is "You have a great day too!"

I realized that there is another problem with the phrase "Hanging in there." I was really just describing exactly what my suit was doing in the closet. My suit, however, also got the benefit of mothballs so moths would not eat through the suit.

I started getting bored with these interactions, and I wanted to do a little bit better than "Hanging in there." One day, I decided to try out something different last year. It was around Thanksgiving time. It was sort of a scientific experiment.

"How are you doing?" someone politely asks me.

I was ready. I was not going to give the standard response that everyone always delivers. My response was going to be a bit different:

"I am doing fantastic, absolutely amazing! I really believe that it is not humanly possible to be doing any better than I am doing at this very moment in time! I had been on cloud sixteen, and it was too cold and too many airplanes! Now, I am on cloud nine. It is absolute and complete perfection! It feels like I am walking through the fields of Shangri-la, and I am also positioned right in the epicenter of Nirvana, and yet I have completely relinquished all desire to obtain a feeling of enlightenment. I sincerely believe that if you studied my mind to discover the true secrets of happiness, and you figured out what was happening inside, you would win the Nobel Prize in science!"

Once I started giving this slightly more positive response to the "how are you doing" question, I started to notice that people genuinely believe I am doing as well as I am saying. I started to believe it too. Even more surprising, when I ask people how they are doing, they replied that they too were doing much better than a few weeks before, when I simply gave the standard response of "Hanging in there!"

It definitely began to catch on. People around the office were all of a sudden feeling better. People have been going out of their way to ask me how I am doing, just because my answer made them feel better.

I was able to get away with this positive attitude at the office, given the positive effect it had on people. Yet, I knew that there was one simple phrase I could not able to use to describe how I was feeling.

"Feeling groovy."

"Feeling Groovy," of course, is the name of a Simon & Garfunkel song that was a big hit in the 1960's. Many years later, there is no one left that feels groovy anymore. In fact, if I would tell people that I was feeling groovy, they would think I was having a psychotic episode.

This is the office talk around the water cooler that we would hear:

"Why are they taking Steve away in a straight-jacket?"

"He said that he was feeling groovy."

"Oh no! That is terrible. Will he be okay?"

"I do not think so. I hear that when someone feels groovy, they put that person away in a mental institution."

"Poor Steve. I just hope I never feel groovy."

"Me, too!"

This all reminded me of when I was a teenager growing up in the Bronx. It was a tough neighborhood. Nevertheless, we did not drink, smoke, or do drugs. What we did do was go to Amy P's house, both boys and girls. We would cram into her bedroom while she played the Carpenters' greatest hits album, and we would all sing the songs. We would all scream the lyrics to "On Top of the World" at the top of our lungs.

> Such a feelin's comin' over me.
> There is wonder in most everything I see.
> Not a cloud in the sky; got the sun in my eyes,
> And I won't be surprised if it's a dream.
>
> Everything I want the world to be
> Is now comin' true especially for me.
> And the reason is clear; it's because you are here.
> You're the nearest thing to heaven that I've seen.
>
> I'm on the top of the world, lookin' down on creation,
> And the only explanation I can find
>
> Is the love that I've found ever since you've been around.
> Your love's put me at the top of the world.
>
> Somethin' in the wind has learned my name.
> And it's tellin' me that things are not the same.
> In the leaves on the trees and the touch of the breeze,
> There's a pleasin' sense of happiness for me.

When we all get together every Thanksgiving, we do not forget all the CrankaTsuris there is in the world. Nevertheless, let us stop and be grateful for just a moment and bring our "Top of the World" game to the table. You will be surprised at how quickly everyone will want to join you.

"Life, I love you. Always groovy."

SHOOT THE MESSENGER CRANKATSURIS

There are many sayings we use every day that we say without thinking. We continue to repeat these sayings despite the fact that they make no real sense whatsoever. One example is "Close, but no cigar!" Why a cigar? What about a pack of cigarettes? On the other hand, what if I do not smoke. Maybe, I do not even like cigars? What if I just get whatever is behind door number three?

Another example is "That is all she wrote." Well, maybe she wrote more. How do we really know? Are you saying that she did not write enough? Obviously, he did not write anything. I do not see you complaining about his writing skills!

That is a saying that goes back to World War II. The military men were fighting on the front in Europe, and they would get letters from their loved ones. They would read their letters out-loud to each other. Some men would get lengthy love letters. They would go on and on how a lifetime passes with each breath not shared, and attached to the letter was a stack of love poems that fully expressed the love that can only found in a lover's heart.

Other men on the front would get a short letter that may say,

"Dear, Steve, I hope you are alive. Having a great time with Johnny! Did I say Johnny? No, I meant Joanna. See you whenever! M."

Then, everyone would gather around Steve and say, "Is that all she wrote?"

Yet, there is one saying that we use that actually makes a whole lot of sense: "Don't shoot me! I am only the messenger!" That is certainly a fair request. There are no saying like "Keep the messenger alive! We have to shoot the person who gave this poor messenger the message!" Of course, that would make much more sense.

Unfortunately, the person who is the author of the message is out of harm's way. The messenger is the only poor schmuck that always is in immediate danger of being the one that is shot.

The poor messenger delivers the message. Immediately, he or she is quickly riddled with CrankaTsuris bullets. "Oh yeah! Blah the blah the blah! I do not believe this blah the blah the blah! You go back and tell that bum exactly this: 'Blah the blah the blah, and you know where you can take your own blah the blah the blah! You shove that blah the blah the blah you know where!'"

After this episode, the messenger goes back to the first person, and delivers the message. Sure enough, there are more CrankaTsuris bullets. The messenger crawls out from this back and forth and barely comes out alive.

We have all had the experience of being the messenger. Now, I am sure you are all anxious to learn how to solve this problem. How can we finally stop shooting the messenger? This is just not fair.

Believe it or not, I will take a contrarian (but perfectly logical) view here and say that we should just go ahead and shoot the messenger. You may think that this is not logical, since the messenger is only the messenger. What about the person who gave the messenger the message? Where is the fairness here? Now that is the problem. The person who says he or she is only the messenger takes a cop out when they say that they are only the messenger.

Why? This is what happens: The messenger receives the message from person one and it says, "Tell Johnny, 'Goblidi gook, goblidi gook, goblidi gook,' and make sure you emphasize a big pile of crap, and don't forget conveying a whole bunch of baloney."

Now, the messenger, if he or she was actually thinking, may point out that the pile of crap and the person who will get this bunch of baloney will not be very happy with the message either.

Instead of being honest in dealing with this, the response is usually akin to this: "Sir, that was insightful, thought provoking, and may I add, beautifully said. If this were a speech, it would go down as one of the greatest speeches in history. Please allow me to be direct when I say this: 'I only wish that my father had shared such words of wisdom with me when I was a child. If he had, I am certain that I would have amounted to much more in life than the position of a lowly messenger!'"

The messenger then delivers the message in exactly that tone. The messenger conveys in their voice this misplaced belief that he or she is in fact delivering words of wisdom, and that, it will be well received by the person who gets the message.

I, for one, do not want any harm, especially CrankaTsuris harm, to have befallen upon any messenger. Messengers certainly do not deserve it. However, the message is not very well received, and once again, the person receiving the message immediately shoots the messenger once again. And, to me, it makes perfect sense that this person shoots the messenger.

Here is where I have to share some of my own personal life experience that ultimately brings me to this conclusion. I spend much of my time at my day job doing negotiations, and with many negotiations, we retain a mediator to work through the issues between the parties.

Mediators do not come cheap. The most sought after mediators can charge as high as a thousand dollars an hour. Even mediocre mediators typically bill between three hundred to five hundred dollars per hour.

Great mediators provide valuable insight, and can take information from an adversarial perspective, and deftly repackage it in a neutral way, and that helps to move the needle on both sides.

Bad mediators just carry the buckets of water back and forth between the parties. They come into each room and they repeat back everything that conveyed to the mediator in the other room. You may imagine that after six or seven hours of this, it gets a bit tired. I get frustrated. At this point, I let out a blistering CrankaTsuris. Taken aback by my onslaught, the mediator shoots back sheepishly "Do not shoot me! I am only the messenger."

The problem that I have is that if I want a messenger, I can get one for fifteen dollars an hour. Twenty-five dollars, tops. I am paying this messenger many times more than that!

The lesson here is a simple one. If the messenger does not want to be shot; the messenger should always think a little bit more about the message they are delivering. Messengers, you see, are rarely only messengers.

CHAPTER 36

BATMAN AND ROBIN CRANKATSURIS

Growing up as a child in the 1960's, I looked forward every week to my favorite TV show: Batman! I loved the choreographed fights. I loved the tongue in cheekiness. I loved how they played their characters so seriously. I loved Alfred the Butler.

My favorite part was actually watching Batman and Robin go down the Bat Pole. How neat was that! All they had to do was slide down a pole to the Bat Cave, and they came down perfectly dressed for action. Their hair was perfect. They never got an upset stomach going down the pole. It did not seem to make them sweaty. Their clothes were perfectly cleaned and ironed. Even more cool was that they never had to worry about what happens if they go out chasing the villains of Gotham City, and that caused them to be a bit late for dinner.

While I did love the show, it was still a bit traumatizing for me. Every week, the Dynamic Duo located the villains in some warehouse along the river. They climbed up the wall of the warehouse with their Bat Rope, jumped in, and then start a fight with all the hired goons, who always had the cutest uniforms. I loved the Riddler's gang of goons the best, dressed up in one piece outfits with lots of question marks covering their bodies.

Just when you thought, they were finished with the last "Pow" and "Kaboom" on twenty goons they took on, down comes the net. Before you can say "Holy Bat Trap", the Caped Crusader and the Boy Wonder are lying helpless underneath the net.

We then watch the next scene in horror. Batman and Robin are tied up to a conveyer belt which either will go into this sawing machine to slice them nicely in half, or it would lead they would get dumped in a vat of boiling oil.

This is not a pretty picture for an eight year old's heroes. During this time, Robin, the Boy Wonder, is freaking out.

"Holy Death Trap!! Batman!!", Robin cries.

The announcer then raises the question on what the next week may bring. Will Batman and Robin end up as Superhero Tempura? Or, will our heroes end up as shoestring or steak potato fries? Stay tuned. Same Bat Time, and Same Bat Channel.

I wait anxiously for the following week to arrive, worried about the Dynamic Duo. The show begins with Robin, once again, freaking out. However, Batman reminds Robin that he happens to have a utility belt. He always manages to get a hand free because Super Villains are never good at tying people's hands up. He gets some awesome tool from his utility belt. I do mean an awesome tool. He could pull out some remote control device that can connect electronically with the conveyor belt and shut down the belt. We are really talking about cool 21st Century technology back in 1968.

A feeling of relief came over me, but I was somewhat disturbed, especially after going through a few villains over the course of a season. I asked myself, "how come it was only Batman that got to have a utility belt". Robin never had a utility belt.

Even to an eight year old, it seemed quite irresponsible for Batman not to provide Robin, a teenager who has to miss school to fight crime, with a utility belt. Batman spends millions of dollars on that fancy Bat Cave, and the Bat Mobile. Yet, he could not afford to get Robin a lousy Utility Belt. How much does one cost? No more than $15. He probably can get a used one for $10. Batman is just a bad employer. He did not even bother to get health or life insurance for Robin.

They do not tell you about this stuff, but it is all true. We never want to tarnish the reputation of our heroes. But folks, let us face the facts. Batman was a cheapskate.

As the season went on, there was another thing about this show that really bothered me. Every other week, they paraded one villain after another, and they all did the same thing. With the Joker, it was the net. With the Riddler, it was the net. With the Penguin, it was the net. Cat Woman had a net. The Mad Hatter, the Black Widow, and King Tut all had amazing nets. Even Egghead had a serviceable net. The only villain without a net was Mr. Freeze. Mr. Freeze would freeze them. Yes. What a surprise that was!

Maybe Batman and Robin did not know about the net the Joker used in the first episode. Maybe, they did not expect the net with the Cat Woman in episode three, two weeks later. Maybe, they honestly thought that the police confiscated the net as they were carrying away the Joker. For the first few weeks, I gave them the benefit of the doubt. They are young, and they do not know any better. Nets are probably a problem only for older super heroes anyway.

However, after a while, this net problem itself gets a bit old. Batman and Robin represent themselves as professional crime fighters. It is in the Superhero best practices handbook they get in Superhero School. Rule number one. Check the ceiling to see if there are any nets hanging above your head.

You mean to tell me that Alfred could not have warned them as they were leaving the Bat Cave. "Watch out for the net, Master Wayne!"

Thankfully, these shows provide great lessons for our CrankaTsuris practice. Ask yourself how many times you had a CrankaTsuris, and the only reason you had one was that you did not have your utility belt. Ask yourself what you would have put in your utility belt. Here is an easy one. You have a CrankaTsuris because it is hot, and you are thirsty. The utility belt could have been a bottle of water.

Here is an even better one. There is a pandemic going around, and you end up getting sick with a mean virus. That will give you a bad CrankaTsuris. Now, if you only had a mask tucked inside your utility belt!

While we are on the topic of pandemics and viruses, and the CrankaTsuris they cause, Batman and Robin reminds us that we should always look up. We learn from not only our own mistakes, but the mistakes of others as well. Many heroes out there forget to look up. They end up trapped in their own net. They did not have a utility belt to save them.

Thankfully, we all watched the show. So, when we go down the Bat Pole to the Bat Cave, we can be ready and prepared. The Joker will not have a chance.

By the way, Batgirl always wore a utility belt.

37

A CRANKATSURIS CHANUKAH

Growing up in the Bronx, I had many non-Jewish friends, and I looked forward to going over to their apartments in December to see their Christmas trees all decorated and lit up. Being Jewish, we did not have Christmas trees. I got even more confused when my non-Jewish friends would ask to come over to my place to see my Chanukah bush. I did not have a Chanukah bush. None of my other Jewish friends had a Chanukah bush. I never even heard of a Chanukah bush.

I do understand that Moses spoke to God as a burning bush on the journey from Egypt. So if we all decided to have a Passover bush, I would be all for that! I can understand that. We can then set it on fire and have amazing conversations talking to our burning bush during the Passover Seder. Finally, we will have the Four Questions answered.

Of course, this was Chanukah. There is no bush in the story of Chanukah. Okay. So maybe, the Macabees hid behind bushes when they fought the Romans. But, the holiday is called the Festival of Lights. They do not call it the Festival of the Bush!

Besides that, I found it to be rather insulting. What are they trying to tell me? "Here is my big beautiful Christmas tree! Now, when can I come over to see your measly little bush?" Do you really think anyone would go to Rockefeller Center to see a teeny tiny little Chanukah bush all lit up?

On top of that, my mother and all the other Jewish mothers would say, "Don't go playing in the bushes!" Now, being Jewish sons, we did not always listen to our mothers.

My friend Marty's mom would say, "Marty, don't go playing in the bushes!" Marty went into the bushes and he got punctures by many pointy thorns! He looked like he went through extreme acupuncture therapy. As poor Marty walked home, people in the neighborhood called animal control to the scene because everyone thought there was a giant porcupine stalking the neighborhood.

My friend Howie's mom would say, "Howie, don't go playing in the bushes!" Now, Howie's favorite food is pizza. If Howie required feeding through an intravenous feeding tube, they would have to figure out how to get the slice of pizza into the tube. One day, he was eating a very oily slice, and it slipped from his hands. The slice of pizza landed straight on top of the head of a giant rat. The rat scurried into the bushes, and Howie went after the rat. Howie was determined and mad. No rat would steal his slice of pizza! When Howie tried to retrieve his slice, the rat bit his hand very hard. Poor Howie was not able to hold a slice of pizza for a week!

My friend Stewie's mom would say, "Stewie, don't go playing in the bushes!" Stewie went to play in the bushes. A skunk was hiding in the bushes, and poor Stewie ended up sprayed by the skunk. He smelled so bad that he had to stay in a bath with Clorox bleach for an entire day. They had to bleach him to get out the smell!

My mom would always tell me, "Stevie, don't go playing in the bushes! Remember what happened to Marty, Howie, and Stewie?" I did remember, and I was not going to go anywhere near the bushes! We played hide-and-go-seek, and the bushes would not be my hiding spot.

Unfortunately, one day, I was hiding behind a garbage can, and flying out of the garbage can, a giant bee flew up and stung me. The bee would not let go of my arm as his stinger teeth clenched tightly on to my elbow. I tried to get away from the bee and ran into the bushes. The bee would not let go until I got the bee stuck on one of the thorns in the bush. Unfortunately, it was a poison ivy bush, and I got bad poison ivy on my arm. I still had poison ivy a full month later! Out of desperation, I rubbed my arm on Stewie's bleached arm, and the poison ivy finally went away!

This is the point: nobody has fond and warm memories about their times in the bushes. A Christmas tree is usually an evergreen pine or fir tree. They are all very pretty, and they smell amazing together with the burning logs of a fireplace that you sit next to stay warm in the winter. However, if you look around, there are many different kinds of other trees! We should not get a bush for Chanukah. We should get our own special tree!

One Chanukah, when I was older, I went to Florida to visit my parents, and it hit me—a Palm tree! My parents would always tell me that, once we get old, we end up retiring in Florida to sit under a palm tree anyway!

The Jewish people should celebrate Chanukah with their own special palm tree. I flew home, and immediately bought the biggest palm tree that I could fit into my house! When the blizzard hits and we get two feet of snow, do you think people go to someone's house to see a Christmas tree? No! Not anymore! They all flock to my house and sun themselves under my very special Chanukah Palm tree! This has become the most popular tree on the block!

Oy to the world!

CHAPTER 38

CRANKATSURIS GRIEVANCES

The true definition of a "CrankaTsuris" is the voicing of every single grievance you may have had from the very moment you came out of your mother's womb. It includes not only the unresolved grievances which may trouble you at that very moment, but since you are on a roll, you throw in all the grievances that you no longer have, the ones that have been completely resolved, those you may have even forgot about, and of course, the ones you didn't even know existed.

The other interesting thing about a pure unadulterated CrankaTsuris is that you let out the CrankaTsuris without any belief, thought or expectation that by the mere release of a good old-fashioned CrankaTsuris, all your problems will be resolved. You have no confidence that by releasing the CrankaTsuris that you will be completely heard, and understood.

In fact, it is your previous experience that whenever you release a CrankaTsuris, your CrankaTsuris is completely ignored, you get scolded for having the CrankaTsuris in the first place, or you get into a CrankaTsuris competition with your loved ones at home. If you get into such a competition, it always happens that you end up on the losing side.

This wonderful experience leaves you nauseous, disgusted, and depressed, and you think for a moment that you have nowhere to turn. I can tell you from personal experience that this feeling is the pits. There is no fruit. Just the pits, and not even the good pits. Rotten pits.

Because you feel the need to release a CrankaTsuris, and this experience does not give you the satisfaction you actually desire from your CrankaTsuris release, eventually, you come up with the idea of hiring a professional. You call up a therapist, make the appointment, and because you have agreed to pay this person handsomely, he or she has agreed to listen to your CrankaTsuris for forty-five minutes.

You are ready. You get there on time, and the therapist asks you "what is bothering you?" or "tell me exactly what it is that is on your mind?" "Yes! Perfect question! This therapist is good!" you think to yourself, and for the next forty-five minutes, you let out the best CrankaTsuris, that has been built up inside you. You are excited about the release of this CrankaTsuris, and the much-anticipated help you are going to get. Finally, you exhale, and give the floor to the therapist.

The therapist replies: "That is certainly quite a lot that you are bringing in. Now, when you say all of that, how does that make you feel?" The therapist then interrupts her own question, and says; "Oh, I am sorry. We have run out of time. We can explore all of that next week."

You walk out a bit flustered. You think to yourself "exactly what just happened in there?" "Did I walk in and see the only therapist who happened to have CrankaTsuris virgin ears?" Did I somehow transform myself into Charlie Brown and land inside the Peanuts comic strip in the Sunday papers, and I was talking to my sister, Lucy?" "I just poured out of my soul for forty five minutes straight what I consider to be home grown, artisanal, hand crafted, certified grade A, world class, award winning CrankaTsuris, and is the question "how does that make you feel?" a multiple choice question?"

For everyone who has experienced the common CrankaTsuris, I want to share with everyone something that should not be considered a newsflash. This is not a multiple-choice question. A CrankaTsuris does not feel good. I recall saying something about pits with no fruit. The fact of the matter is that it feels depressing, irritating, annoying, and agitating. How does it feel to listen to someone's CrankaTsuris? Not much better. It feels depressing, irritating, annoying and agitating. In fact, this is probably the reason that this therapist charged you so much in the first place!

Reading this, you may be thinking: "Wait a second. You are all about this effective crankiness thing. You have this CrankaTsuris Method you are trying to get me all hooked on. I am getting a bit confused, not to mention a bit depressed, irritated, annoyed and agitated!"

I understand. But, please remember. The CrankaTsuris has been around for millions and millions of years since the Last Surviving Dinosaur: the TyrantoCrankaTsuris. Even though it has been around for millions of years, the CrankaTsuris itself has only recently been discovered. Now, that we have finally discovered and understand the CrankaTsuris, and know that it happens to afflict every human being on the planet, we are better able to treat it, and minimize its paralyzing effects on the human psyche.

Remember the therapist that ends the session asking the question about how does this makes you feel. We are encouraged to verbalize our feelings; "I feel angry. I feel depressed." Yes. This is very helpful information for the therapist who happens to be the only one with CrankaTsuris virgin ears. However, this will make not you feel better.

Calling this a CrankaTsuris may help. You get to strip away the title of "angry" next to person. You get to strip away the title of "depressed" next to person. You are just a "person" who happens to have a CrankaTsuris, and it is something that we all have in common. Think about it. Do you want the doctor to tell you that you have this very rare incurable disease, or something that everyone gets, and if you get some rest and treatment, it should go away?

You may now ask how exactly this CrankaTsuris goes away. Since the CrankaTsuris is something that is something universally shared by all of humanity, it begins with empathy for ourselves, and it ends with empathy for others.

With all of that empathy circling around us, the CrankaTsuris can slowly disappear.

39

DRIVE ME CRAZY CRANKATSURIS

Chances are that all of us have had this one particularly painful experience:

A chemical reaction in the head goes off as you hear yourself mouthing two sentences, connected to each other, and that goes like this:

"It drives me crazy when"

and

"I cannot understand how."

You never want to have to say these two sentences back to back because it can mean only one thing. You are having an uncontrollable CrankaTsuris. Smoke is coming out of your ears. Your blood pressure is through the roof. You are screaming at the top of your lungs because you are furious. It is definitely not safe to have anyone within ten miles from you.

Well, I had two situations in one day, back to back, that I got to enjoy the pleasure of experiencing.

Just recently, my daughter had a crack in the windshield of her car. I came up to visit, and went with her to the windshield repair shop. After waiting for an hour, the technician installed a new windshield. However, it was only after we drove off that we realized that he installed the wrong windshield. A breeze was coming into the car. Rain was in the forecast for the next day, and the interior would get soaked. We had to turn around.

I was fuming. "It drives me crazy that we go all this way to a specialty store for windshields, and they screw up the one thing that they specialize in! I cannot understand how you can go to a windshield store and they do not know how to install a windshield!"

We confronted the owner, and told him about the problem. He was fuming. He said to us "It drives me crazy when I can't rely on my technicians to install a windshield. Once we take it out, we are unable to use it, and my profit margins are small. I cannot afford such a thing! I cannot understand how my technician screwed up. I showed him the fifteen minute YouTube video on how to do the installation!"

The owner yelled at his technician who proceeded to install the correct windshield. Afterwards, I was in the bathroom stall, and I heard the technician coming in and then talking to another employee. He was fuming.

"It drives me crazy when the boss gives me a hard time for installing a wrong windshield when he does not bother training anybody. I cannot understand how he expects me how to know how to install a windshield from watching a fifteen minute video!"

Finally, the correct windshield was properly installed and since it was getting late, I suggested that we go to a restaurant for dinner. It took twenty minutes to have the waiter take our order. Once he took our order, we waited fifty minutes, and we still did not get any of our food. Everyone who came in and were seated after us were served. Frustrated, I looked everywhere to summon the waiter.

I was fuming. "It drives me crazy when we order food, and I look at every other table getting served except for us. Everyone came in after us no less. I cannot understand how the waiter does not see that we have been waiting forever!"

I finally was able to summon the waiter. The waiter apologized and quickly brought out what we had ordered. However, it was ice cold. We complained, and the waiter told us that the owner would not charge us for the entree.

The owner came out to apologize to us. He was fuming. "I am so sorry. It drives me crazy when something like this happens. I run this restaurant on such low profit margins, and this is so unacceptable. I cannot understand how the waiter can serve all the other tables, and not attend to you. Meanwhile, you were sitting here not getting served for an hour."

I went to the bathroom, and again, I was sitting in the bathroom stall. I overheard the waiter talking to a fellow employee. He was fuming.

"It drives me crazy when the boss is constantly directing me where to go, and then, he gets upset because I have to ignore a table because of his constant directions. I cannot understand how he expects me to wait twenty tables all by myself!"

Oy.

After I experienced this, I noticed that there was a direct correlation between going crazy, and the lack of desire, but not ability, to understand. We all have had an argument with someone, and we try to calm the other person down by saying this:

"Can I explain? I like to make you understand."

Now, when you offer this gift of understanding, most of the time, this offer gets rejected. Understanding is not possible. It is not in the cards. We want to hold to our craziness. We think it is power. However, in reality, it is really holding on to powerlessness.

There is a very simple reason for this. If you let the other person explain, and try to make you understand, do you know what happens? You now have become enabled to make the other person understand why what happened was so hurtful. You can explain how it made you a bit crazy. You create a situation that allows you to be heard by the other person. You have taken some power in this tangle.

Coincidentally, that night, we went back home and watched one of the Batman movies with the Joker and Harvey Dent who became the villain Two Face. Think about this. Can you even have a Batman movie if they never explained how Bruce Wayne became Batman? Or why the villains became who they were?

It turns out that we have a huge thirst for understanding. Then, if we try to open ourselves up to a good dose of understanding, perhaps we would have much less Drive Me Crazy CrankaTsuris.

CRANKATSURIS SIDE EFFECTS

I have been very fortunate to have completed close to fifty marathons over the past twenty years. Since people know that I am a marathon runner, there are two questions that people always ask me. I understand the first question. I do not understand the follow-up one.

The first question that people typically ask me is "How many miles do you run every week?" The answer is typically fifty miles. Then, there is the next question; "How are your knees?"

Thankfully, my knees are just fine. What I do not understand about this question is if I tell someone that I run fifty miles a week, all of a sudden, people have this worry that I must be in some excruciating pain. The unfounded belief that I must be in terrible pain is implied in the question itself. I have never gotten a response to the first answer; "Wow. Your knees must be in great shape!" Even my doctor is concerned. Every year, after I inform her on how much I run, she asks me "how are your knees?"

Just to prove that my knees are just fine, I just hope these people do not expect me to run three or four hundred miles a week. Of course, my knees would be fine, except that by then, they would have fallen off both my legs.

I bring this up because I am closing in on sixty years old. I tuned fifty-nine last week. I learned that, after I turned fifty, I entered the age group that starts to be focused on the topic of pain management. It turns out that everyone in this group has their own personal pain manager.

I have to start by saying that I am not fond of the term "pain manager." The term makes no sense to me. The reason is that when I have pain, I have no interest in having the pain managed. I want the pain eliminated. I want to be pain to be gone, and out of my life. The faster it is gone, the happier I will be.

Compare this term to the term "babysitter." What is a babysitter? A babysitter is someone who comes into your house, and for a few hours, manages both the house and the baby. Nobody hires a babysitter, and instructs the babysitter: "I hope the baby will be gone when we get home!"

Do not worry. The baby should be home when you get back. However, if you get a pain manager, the pain will also likely be there when you get home. Every pain manager tells you a different thing. Try yoga. Try palates. How about the Alexander Technique? Have you heard of Feldenkrais? There are just so many choices.

So, you settle on doing yoga. Again, there are more choices. They tell you to try Hatha Yoga, or maybe Bikram Yoga, or maybe ten other kinds of Yoga. Okay. You finally settle on Bikram. The yoga instructor starts the class by asking if anybody has certain limitations that the instructor should be aware of. You raise your hand, and spend the first ten minutes of the class explaining to the instructor your "top ten" limitation list. The instructor appeared to have shown some mild interest up to limitation number two, and then, appeared to have tuned out. You know that the instructor tuned out because you never received any guidance on how exactly to do the class with these limitations. Wait a second. You did get one instruction.

"Do the best you can."

You go through the class and you find out that you can do one pose. You try not to do another pose. It starts to hurt. You quickly learned that one pose will be good for your legs, but it can hurt your back. You find out that the other pose is good for your back, but it can hurt your legs. You should do Warrior One Pose, but be careful with Warrior Two Pose. If you do Warrior Three Pose, make sure you get back to do more Warrior One to offset any pain caused by Warrior Three.

When yoga fails, you turn to your pain manager, and this manager prescribes for you a variety of pain relief medication. I went hiking with friends the other day, and the two people I was with spent the whole time talking about the side effects of each pain medication they are taking or considering. One prescription may cause vomiting. Another causes diarrhea. One causes dizziness and heart palpitations. Another causes high blood pressure and heart attack. One may cause cancer, and finally, another may cause death.

After listening to this two compare notes for two hours, I could not take it anymore. I blurted out; "These are not side effects? They are effects."

"Death is an effect! It is not something that just passes while you are digesting the pill."

Of course, after you get to the end of the prescription warnings list, it always says:

"If you get any of these side effects, please consult with your physician immediately." Needless to say, I am not sure that if I get this death effect, I will be calling up my physician.

It is an effect. You would never go to a restaurant, and give the waiter this order:

"For my main entree, I would like to get one scoop of the sorbet. Bring two spoons because we are sharing. As for the side dish, I will have the forty-eight ounce cowboy bone-in ribeye for two. Do not worry. I can finish this all by myself. Last week, I did the porterhouse for three!"

The point here is that we try to minimize the effects by simply calling them side effects. If something becomes minimized, we do not have to take that thing seriously. If they are side effects, they appear to be much smaller, and even more manageable. Even if the side effect is death, they convince you that it would not be permanent, and you probably will be able to get over it quickly.

However, what I am concerned with here is our CrankaTsuris. If we look at the common CrankaTsuris, and we want to begin to embrace effective crankiness, there are no such thing as side effects. Everything is an effect. Some effects can ruin your day or week. Other effects are long lasting and have severe consequences. Some effects can be pain to your loved ones.

When we appreciate the effects, and know that they are not side effects, we begin to take the causes more seriously. We examine what the cause is, and once we understand the cause more completely, we then come up with different strategies on how we can manage our CrankaTsuris.

Yes. This is where management is perfectly fine. This is where management is required. When we start utilizing our strategies, we are on the path to effective crankiness.

41

THE FIVE-STEP APPROACH TO EFFECTIVE CRANKINESS

Throughout this book, I have laid out various strategies to effective crankiness or what I have coined "the CrankaTsuris Method." Here, I like to lay out the five steps you can employ to lay down the foundation, and begin your own journey to effective crankiness.

1. Rename your crankiness as a CrankaTsuris.

The crankiness comes in all different kind of forms. It come from anger. It comes from fear. It comes from frustration. It comes from depression. These are just a few. The problem we all face with the crankiness is that it creates a chaotic mind.

These are real feelings, and many times, these negative feelings turn into negative thoughts. The negative thoughts in our mind then want to be fed. Because of this, we begin to create stories to allow those feelings to grow. Suppose, I am feeling angry toward a person for one thing that person did, I can then start thinking of three other things that never happened. I do that because it keeps that adrenalin of anger growing. We then want to take actions because of these feelings, and too many of those actions are harmful to ourselves and to others.

With these feelings, there is no ground, and no real feeling of control. The actions we take are typically bad choices because there is no ground, and no control. These are acts of impulsiveness.

Roll all these feelings up and deposit all those feelings into your chest and when you feel it there, think of it as something that takes shape. You can picture in your mind any shape that suits you, and this will be your CrankaTsuris.

2. Think of your CrankaTsuris" exactly in the same was as you would think of a virus and be aware that what you have is the "Common CrankaTsuris."

Nobody likes it when he or she gets a cold. However, nobody really freaks out when a person gets one. Why? It is because there was some person was smart enough a long time ago to call it the common cold even though there are people, for some reason, never even get a cold.

Since we all have our own CrankaTsuris on a daily basis, think of it as the Common CrankaTsuris." We are not dealing with some incurable cancer that you will need rounds of chemotherapy. It will pass. More importantly, while you are dealing with the Common CrankaTsuris, you can look around the room filled with people, and the infection rate is likely close to 100 percent.

There is something about not being alone that grounds us and gives us a bit of comfort. If I am feeling I am all alone in this, I am only looking inwards, and the world outside is the enemy. If I am not alone, I start looking outside and feeling compassion for this around me, and then something happens. I begin to have more compassion for myself.

3. Create a mutual CrankaTsuris support team.

Get your friends and family to buy into the CrankaTsuris concept. This takes the concept of the Common CrankaTsuris to the next level. This will be the point that everyone can embrace his or her crankiness and the crankiness of his or her loved ones. This is when we start to know when to self-diagnose the CrankaTsuris, and even help diagnose the CrankaTsuris of our loved ones. We all agree to support each other when we have the bouts of CrankaTsuris. We are all doctors who know how to treat this.

Think about what happens. I may actually be having a CrankaTsuris because of something you did was annoying. Before, I would go on the attack because of this annoyance. You may then feel to attack back or become defensive. If we have the approach that we give space and treat the CrankaTsuris as if we are all doctors, we are being responsive to the CrankaTsuris, and we are not getting all personal with it. It becomes clear when your partner or everyone on your support team gets to do this. Everyone knows that he or she will get the same treatment in return. Everyone will also see that things do not get as escalated into a crisis as it once did.

The more that everyone participates, the more effective we all become in our CrankaTsuris practice. Eventually, this may be the part of the day that each of us can all look forward to.

4. Practice your CrankaTsuris when you are not cranky.

Eventually, the CrankaTsuris practice will be something you can have fun doing. It should be able to make you laugh. However, if you will be self-diagnosing and providing treatment for the CrankaTsuris, it is good to get some practice. Make believe you are practicing giving CPR. Make believe you are doing improvisational theater, and everyone is a performer. Make believe that you are all training for the Tsuris Olympics. Only one person can get the gold medal.

5. Make sure you have a quiet place when you need quiet.

While much of this is letting out the CrankaTsuris in a healthy way and in a supportive environment, it is also necessary that everyone have his or her quiet place. If you are feeling completely depleted, and you need to go into a corner, that is where you should go. However, getting back to the support team, everybody gets a quiet place, and everybody gives each other the quiet time that they need.

<u>Bonus Rule</u>: Spend every day finding things to marvel about.

I remember an experience that I had as a child. I was given my first seashell to examine. I marveled at the shape of the seashell. I marveled at the colors of the seashell. I marveled at the sound of the ocean that I was able to hear just by putting the shell next to my ear. I marveled at the fact that this shell even existed.

We are told all too often to be grateful for what we have. We should be thankful. There is no argument with that. However, too often, there is a "should be" attached to being thankful. It becomes something that has a feeling of being forced upon you.

The great thing of taking a few moments of every day to marvel at something is that you get to decide. You have sole ownership of your own marvel. Nobody tells a child to marvel at a seashell. They do not have to. Soon, the marvel of the child quickly turns to delight.

Chances are that if you marvel at enough things every day, you will soon find that you getting to experience a marvelous day.

You are on your way.

EPILOGUE
A TRIBUTE TO MY MOM AND MY DAD

I wrote the TyrantoCrankaTsuris story six months after my mother, a Holocaust survivor, passed away in September 2017, on the first day of Rosh Hashanah, one of the most holy days of the year. I am a long-distance runner, and while stories always somehow flew into my head, in the months after my mom passed away, I could only hear her voice. It was a syrupy voice. She never talked in conversational tones, but rather in proclamations. There was always a slight pause between the phrasing, for perfect comedic timing. She was the Yogi Berra of Jewish mothers.

"Where you put it … that's where you'll find it!"

"Why did I make so much … if you are not going to eat?"

"I talk to you … like I talk to a wall."

"Don't be a hero … wear a hat!"

"If you say so … it is so."

And the best saying was in Yiddish: "Don't be a *Moyshe Groyce* with *zserrissena gatkas!*" That means, "Don't be the great Moses with torn underwear!"

In *The Last Surviving Dinosaur: The TyrantoCrankaTsuris*, there are three bully dinosaurs, and the TyrantoCrankaTsuris, with her cranking out all her tsuris, makes these bully dinosaurs disappear. She is a heroic figure. She used her voice. So many people during the Holocaust did not have their voices heard. They all could have used a TyrantoCrankaTsuris.

The father in the story reminds his daughter that this is power.

She was given the power of words, the power of having a voice. But, with a voice, I am also reminded of my Zen practice, and my Zen teacher, who always uses the phrase "utilizing skillful means." That is having real power.

I heard my mother's voice, and I wrote a book so her sweet and very funny voice will be heard. It was written with the hope that people who feel they have no voice should seek it out. When I sign a book for a child, I make sure to sign it with the phrase "Never be afraid to take on all those bigger and badder dinosaurs!"

Never be afraid to use your voice.

There is or more thing. In this book about "effective crankiness," ultimately love will always be the answer. On February 5, 2020, my father passed away three days after his ninety-third birthday. I was going through old pictures and found an extraordinary undated note my mother wrote to my father. She expressed in the note something I never heard her say out loud. Especially because my mom was a holocaust survivor, it was the best and most meaningful gift I ever got from her, hearing her voice once again:

> *"Because I love you, I wish I could tell you all the joy your love has brought. But maybe, Dear, you will find a hint with this loving thought. You have shown me life is beautiful in ways I never knew, and my world is so much happier just because of you, my darling! Happy birthday from your loving wife Rose."*

ABOUT THE AUTHOR

Steven Joseph is the author of *The Last Surviving Dinosaur: The TyranCrankaTsuris*. He regularly blogs on issues of crankiness on www.StevenJosephAuthor.com. He is also an attorney and lives in Hoboken, New Jersey.

CPSIA information can be obtained
at www.ICGtesting.com
Printed in the USA
LVHW050520171220
674382LV00001B/1

9 781480 893818